PETRONIUS THE ARTIST

Essays on the Satyricon

and its Author

by

H. D. RANKIN

MARTINUS NIJHOFF / THE HAGUE

PETRONIUS THE ARTIST

PETRONIUS THE ARTIST

Essays on the Satyricon and its Author

by

H. D. RANKIN

MARTINUS NIJHOFF / THE HAGUE / 1971

ISBN 90 247 5020 2

PRINTED IN THE NETHERLANDS

To my wife

PREFACE

With one exception, the essays which form this book have appeared in various Classical periodicals. They do not claim to present a comprehensive account of Petronius and his work, but are intended to illustrate by discussion some aspects of the work and its author that seem, to me at least, to be of interest.

"Did Tacitus quote Petronius" appeared in *L'Antiquité Classique* XXXVII, 2, 1968, 641–643; "On Tacitus' Biography of Petronius" and "Petronius, Priapus and Priapeum LXVIII" in *Classica et Mediaevalia* XXVI 1–2, 1965, 233–245, and XXVII 1–2, 1966, 225–242 respectively; "Some Comments on Petronius' Portrayal of Character" will appear soon in *Eranos*; "Eating People is Right" appeared in *Hermes* 97 Bd., 3, 1969, 381–384; "Some Themes of Concealment and Pretence in Petronius' *Satyricon*" in *Latomus* Tome XXVIII, 1, 1969, 99–119; and "Petronius, A Portrait of the Artist" in *Symbolae Osloenses* XLV, 1970, 118–128. I wish to thank the editors of these periodicals for their permission to reproduce the articles.

Professor J. P. Sullivan was kind enough to let me see the proofs of his book: *The Satyricon of Petronius, A Literary Study* (London, 1968) before it was published. I acknowledge this with thanks.

I wish to acknowledge permission from The Bodley Head to quote from F. Scott Fitzgerald's *Tender is the Night, Bodley Head Scott Fitzgerald*, Vol. II p. 91.

I wish to thank Mrs. A. Brodie for typing the material, and Mrs. L. Andrew for her help with the proofs.

Monash University

CONTENTS

PETRONIUS, A PORTRAIT OF THE ARTIST

In its essentials the story is familiar: A brilliant man at a tyrant's court: a man for whom it is difficult to write anything but satire. He enjoys his short period of glory, the discovery of his administrative gifts[1] which run in team with his analytical talent as a writer; then comes the diversion of his career from its apparently purposeful direction as pro-consul of Bithynia, then as consul; his closer contacts with the court as arbiter of elegance,[2] then his downfall, caused by a jealous and criminally minded rival.[3] Slander was too readily believed. His protective colouration of *simplicitas*[4] was of no avail, for in the examination of all that he had said or done, the worst interpretation easily was made to prevail. Nothing remained but the suicide that had become the customary exit for the disaffiliated intellectual in the early empire.

This in brief is Tacitus' account. He has more to say; and what he says suggests that he admired, or at least noted the career of an extraordinary individual; or perhaps that he was interested enough to follow in his account a source that admired him.[5] Tacitus tells us further

[1] Tac. *Annales* XVI, 18, 3: *proconsul tamen Bithyniae et mox consul vigentem se ac parem negotiis ostendit.*

[2] Tac. *Annales* XVI, 18: *inter paucos familiarium Neroni adsumptus est elegantiae arbiter, dum nihil amoenum et molle adfluentia putat nisi quod ei Petronius adprobavisset.*

[3] Tac. *Annales* XVI, 51, 6; XV 50, 4; 59, 3 etc.

[4] Tac. *Annales* XVI, 18, 2: *ac dicta factaque eius quanto solutiora et quandam sui neglegentiam praeferentia, tanto gratius in speciem simplicitatis accipiebantur.* It is difficult to decide how much significance should be attributed to this phrase's key word *simplicitas*, or whether the occurrence of the word in Petr. 132 has a "programmatic" function, as has been maintained. Clearly some kind of archaic quality is referred to; see Stubbe, *Philologus*, suppl. bd. 25, 150-1: Rogner, *Hermes*, 1951, 223-4, Bickel, *RhM* XC, 1941. 269-72; J. P. Sullivan, *The Satyricon of Petronius, A Literary Study*, London 1968, 99 note, 1.

[5] K. F. C. Rose, "The Author of the Satyricon," *Latomus* XX, 1961, 811-25 argued that the source was Cluvius Rufus: I have tried to suggest it was Fannius, *infra* 94-99.

that this man, this apparent aesthete and socialite that turned night into day and said so many self-exposing, self-mocking things, committed a final joke against society by parodying the Stoic oppositionists' pompous style of suicide.[6] No platitudes for him, no attempts to outdo Plato's *Phaedo* in the delineation of noble death. He chose popular songs and a good dinner, and then slept away with his veins open.[7] (He had coolly had them opened and rebound before he began to dine.) Not only did he mock the philosophic suicide, he mocked the role almost of Court Fool that he had played himself, and in his last testament[8] he executed a severe enough revenge on the *princeps* who had been so easily stirred against him by Tigellinus. Tacitus approved of Petronius' way of dying and does not seem to have disapproved of his manner of life. The contrast of apparent idleness and evident efficiency is an old commonplace, which we can see applied (in a slightly different sense) in Cicero's *De Officiis* to the *otium* of Africanus.[9] It is an aristocratic theme, close to the old hatred of βαναυσία, echoed in a democratised form in Pericles' "Funeral Oration,"[10] elevated to a principle in Plato's notion of the philosopher "guardian" of the state. It is essentially anti-tragical, and in the words of contemporary "beat" philosophers, it would be called "cool".[11] In similar terms, Seneca's death would need to be "hot." Tacitus liked the "coolness" of Petronius. He chose to mention also the testament of Nero's vices which Petronius composed before his death, and omitted to mention the *Satyricon*.[12]

---

[6] Seneca's death: Tac. *Annales* XV, 63; 64, 4: *postremo stagnum calidae aquae introiit, respergens proximos servorum addita voce libare se liquorem illum Iovi liberatori.* cf. the death of Thrasea, Tac. *Annales* XVI, 35, 2.

[7] Tac. *Annales* XVI, 19, 2: *neque tamen praeceps vitam expulit, sed incisas venas, ut libitum, obligatas aperire rursum et adloqui amicos, non per seria aut quibus gloriam constantiae peteret. audiebatque referentis nihil de immortalitate animae et sapientium placitis, sed levia carmina et facilis versus.*

[8] Tac. *Annales* XVI, 19, 5: *ne codicillis quidem, quod plerique pereuntium, Neronem aut Tigellinum aut quem alium potentium adulatus est, sed flagitia principis sub nominibus exoletorum feminarumque et novitatem cuiusque stupri perscripsit atque obsignata misit Neroni.*

[9] On the *otium* of Africanus, Cicero *De Off* I, i; *De Rep* I, xvii,27.

[10] Thucydides II, 40: Φιλοκαλοῦμέν τε γὰρ μετ' εὐτελείας καὶ φιλοσοφοῦμεν ἄνευ μαλακίας. πλούτῳ τε ἔργου μᾶλλον καιρῷ ἢ λόγου κόμπῳ χρώμεθα, καὶ τὸ πένεσθαι οὐχ ὁμολογεῖν τινὶ αἰσχρόν, ἀλλὰ μὴ διαφεύγειν ἔργῳ αἴσχιον.

[11] Marshall McLuhan, *Understanding Media* 1964; L. Lipton, *The Holy Barbarians*, N.Y. 1959.

[12] Tac. *Annales* XVI, 18, 2: *ac dicta factaque;* R. Syme, *Tacitus*, Oxford 1958, 336 n. 5 suggests that the *Satyricon* might be implied in this phrase: which is theoretically possible in that it is a frequently repeated set phrase of general import: *Annales* I, 72, 11; III, 50, 7; IV, 71, 15; VI, 24, 3; *Agr* 46, 9; *Hist.*

What we know of Tigellinus, the efficient cause of Petronius' downfall, suggests an antithesis to Petronius. He was a brutal and base personality, aggressive, treacherous, with a hatred of philosophers and intellectuals that was in some sense the counterpart of an almost superstitious dread of them.[13] His transactions with Apollonius of Tyana illustrate this well: the superstition of a gangster. Tacitus' description of Tigellinus' death contrasts with that of Petronius: it is the example of a bad and squalid end.[14] Petronius had his own form of anti-intellectualism, – in him it emerged as a distaste for the rhetorical and philosophical conventions which prevailed in his time, and which he thought should be countered by a kind of classicism. He himself, the originator of a unique style, did not follow this, but it formed the basis of that individuality as a writer which has been regarded in his case as an approximate Atticism.[15] At all events, both in form and subject-matter, his work tells us something of the general low ebb of intellectual life in his time; quite apart from his explicit strictures of contemporary writers, his own style by its implications, and his description of anomic society in itself, achieve a refutation of what he saw before his eyes as the standard literary practice. Also, his manner of death makes its own comment. But this does not preempt the question of his general purpose in writing the *Satyricon*, a purpose which we cannot easily define for lack of evidence.

K. F. C. Rose argued that the author of the *Satyricon* was T. Petronius Niger,[16] and he maintained also that the date of its composition was at least well into 65 A. D.[17] Rose's arguments are strongly but perhaps not ultimately persuasive, though they may be worthy of a provisional acceptance. We know nothing of Petronius' family background, of his social and regional origins; nor do we know whether he had a family, a wife and children.[18] It seems unlikely that surviving spouse or children would not have been mentioned at some point. For Petronius' attitude to the world, we rely, apart from Tacitus, upon the *Satyricon* itself, and a man's writings are often a shaky enough

III, 32, 18; 49, 6; IV, 32, 4; There is no reason to suppose that *dicta* has any special reference to literary composition or *recitatio* in XVI, 18, 2. (nor *facta*).

[13] Consider his dealings with Apollonius: Philostratus, *Apoll. Ty* IV. 44.

[14] Tac. *Hist.* I, 72.

[15] Sullivan 261.

[16] Rose, *op. cit.*

[17] K. F. C. Rose, "The Date of the Satyricon" *Classical Quarterly*, N. S. XIII, 1, 1962, 166-8.

[18] But see Rose, *Lat.* 825; note 5 above.

guide to his mind. At least we learn from them some of his literary opinions, – I think there is no doubt of that – but there is little hard evidence of a serious interest in philosophy. Oscar Raith's suggestion that Petronius' thought was predominantly Epicurean[19] is attractive, but is based upon too few convincing texts. The manner of his death tells us that he was not a Stoic, (or at all events a very strange one); the fact that for purposes of defaming him he could be classed with a predominantly Stoic or Cynic group of the "opposition," does not tell us much more than that he was regarded as an intellectual, capable of self-expression, and therefore potentially dangerous. It does not prove that he was on friendly terms with Stoics or members of the "opposition," nor does it indicate that he was particularly unfriendly. Epicureanism seems to fit the attitude of disengagement which he put forward as a mask, and his death was more Epicurean than anything else.[20] Raith concedes some elements of Cynic influence, but not large ones. His *ignavia*[21] could be either Epicurean or Cynic: his *neglegentia sui*[22] and his delight in saying outrageous, self-incriminating things suggest (superficially) the attitudes of a Cynic. It is possible that Tacitus knew of him from a Cynic influenced source such as the biographer Fannius, which would explain the Cynic traces.[23] In fact, there is no reason to regard him as a serious philosopher at all. Possibly he had some systematic acquaintance with the great philosophies, – equally possible he had not, but simply drew upon an "atmospheric" acquaintance with their main themes.[24] He was more artist than philosopher.

In looking at the *Satyricon*, a reader might easily be excused if he wondered how Petronius managed to survive after its publication. If Rose's view of when it was written is correct, he did not survive for long, but his mask of simplicity must have helped him to escape an immediate backlash of hostility. Probably the work was composed episodically for recitation to a select group of friends of court circles, and it is reasonable to suppose that Nero was kept sweet by the fact that he was a member, indeed, the patron of this "ingroup" of con-

---

[19] O. Raith, *Petronius ein Epikureer*, Diss. Erlangen 1963.

[20] The Epicureans withdrew from life unobtrusively, *tanquam e theatro*, Cicero *De Fin* I, 15, 44: Lucretius III, 944.

[21] Tac. *Annales* XVI, 18, 1: this word has the possible suggestion of ἀταραξία cf. note 22 below.

[22] Tac. *Annales* XVI, 18, 2; both words might suggest ἀναιδεία and παρρησία cf. my discussion, 94, n.18 and 97, n. 25.

[23] Refs. at note 5 above.

[24] 104, 132.

noisseurs. For it is not easy to see how Nero could safely have been left out of the group of people who were aware of the *Satyricon*. An attractive argument in favour of the view that he was in fact left out, resides in the thesis that he accepted so readily Tigellinus' innuendos about Petronius because a rumour about the *Satyricon* had reached him, arousing his suspicions in advance and preparing the ground for the accusations he was soon to hear about his *arbiter elegantiae*. Such a thesis is not necessary, however, to explain Nero's conduct, for he readily fell into hostility against his friends; had he been kept in the dark about the *Satyricon* and then heard of it by accident, he would probably have treated it as a libel.[25] Yet when Petronius was eventually brought to notice as an alleged political malefactor, – on judicious re-reading or recall, the *Satyricon* could easily have been retrospectively interpreted as *probrosum* or *famosum*, and this would be clinched by the latest testament of the author, which was specific abuse of Nero.

For a time, long or short, Petronius' capacity for ironically praising misers for extravagance[26] would deceive even Nero, or at least give him no occasion where he felt in honour bound to take offence. Nero was not particularly sensitive to satirical abuse in any case; he was prepared to endure a considerable amount of it before taking action. What he seriously disliked was rivalry in the sphere of poetry or acting.[27] Seneca's distinction as a poet gave cause of anger to Nero, who would not endure a rival in this sphere. Sullivan is probably right in thinking that the poem on Troy in Petronius has no connection with the poem on the taking of Troy that Nero is supposed to have recited at the time when Rome was on fire,[28] and that the poem in the *Satyricon* had the more acceptable object of ridiculing Seneca. A retrospective hostile reading of the *Satyricon* after Petronius' disgrace, might suggest something different, and we cannot exclude the notion that Petronius the master of the techniques of σπουδογέλοιον, [29] did not originally have

---

[25] Nero was relatively tolerant of libellous attacks upon him (Suet. *Nero* 38-9) but such attacks could be employed against their perpetrators when occasion demanded: e.g., the cases of Vestinus, Tac. *Annales* XV, 68, 4; Antistius XVI, 21, 2.

[26] Plutarch, "How to tell a flatterer from a friend:" 60 e.

[27] Clearly it was rivalry in poetry rather than prose that irritated Nero's envy: *e.g.* in the case of Seneca, Tac. *Annales* XIV, 52; Lucan, Suet. edit. Roth. Lips 1882, 299-300; see B. W. Henderson's discussion: *The Life and Principate of the Emperor Nero*, London 1903, 163-7, 262-4.

[28] Sullivan 186-189 argues that it is an attack on Seneca's poetry.

[29] A characteristic of Menippus' work: D. R. Dudley, *A History of Cynicism*, London 1937, 76.

some ulterior ridicule of Nero in mind when he wrote. At the time when this piece of the *Satyricon* was recited or otherwise published, Petronius' assumption of simplicity and naïveté might have saved him from the suggestion that he was satirising Nero. His means of fighting, his principal weapon, was this assumed innocence.

Petronius' shatteringly simple-minded style of talking seemed to proceed from the fundamental nihilism of the socialite who is no longer capable of surprise, who coolly speaks unpalatable "truths," not from love of veracity, but in order to smooth out by means of a joke the horrors of life and acclimatise them to the context of polite conversation. At a (usually) different social level, this would be the behaviour that characterised the Cynic. We may ask the question about a man of Petronius' high standing: Who of his sophisticated peers would be shocked at his utterances? It hardly mattered to shock the ordinary people. The circle of Nero's acquaintances would not easily be shocked. The philosophers might take his views in their stride, without much attention to their amorality. We do not know enough of his origins to know whether he was likely to be trying to shock his family and attack their standards. But Roman delight in paradox runs deep;[30] also, an artist who adopts some kind of mask, whether of arrogance, humility, or any other characteristic, need not be consciously aware of what he is doing or why he is doing it, though he may study in precise detail the means needed to effect the impression of his disguise upon others.[31] Furthermore, there was a consensus or conglomerate of accepted standards of behaviour, good and bad, to which even the most hardened courtier would pay lip service. The pleasure of breaking *tabu* comes, at least in part, from an awareness of what it prohibits: what we call "orgy" in a pejorative sense, is a parody of an institution:

---

[30] Contrasts between appearance and reality were tolerated, provided that appearances were maintained: permissiveness in youth Cicero *Pro Caelio* 39-43, 48. (R. G. Austin's note on 48); the dual standards practised by the elder Cato, Aul. Gell. X, 23, XIII, 119.
For Tacitus' delight in the contrasts in human personality: Syme's comments, *op. cit.* 336-8, 548, 553. Contrasts in a person like Catilina were worthy of note: Cicero *Catil.* I. 10; II 5; III 7; *Pro Caelio* 6: Sallust *Catilina* 5.
[31] An illustration of how complicated this subject may be can be had from R. Ellmann's interpretative biography, W. B. Yeats, *Yeats: The Man and the Masks*, London 1961, which pays especial regard to the personae that the poet used in his work: see especially 182 ff. E's discussion of the change in tone in the early years of this century towards a rougher and more outspoken sexuality in his work – a change which brought in new personae with the new material. The use of masks is connected with a need both for the concealment and evolution of the poet's self *cf.* the discussion 174-181.

witness the mock-marriage of Silius and Messalina.[32] Consider also
the reversal of accepted social forms in the *Saturnalia*. Another point
would be that the smart set of Nero's court would realise with a satisfaction that was increased by Tigellinus' jealousy, that in Petronius
they had a collective voice. The acceptance of the informal distinction
arbiter elegantiae, presumably from the *princeps*, was a clear psychological and social gain for the author. In the end, in a strange way,
Petronius' premortuary *diatribe* (if we may call it such) of commination
against those really intimate vices of Nero of which Petronius had no
official knowledge,[33] brings socialite and Cynic preacher together,
face to face in a wry grin.

We shall never know how serious or otherwise Petronius was in the
assumption of the mask that Tacitus describes. It is clear that he was
capable of seeing and interpreting life at more than one level of meaning.
The mode of σπουδογέλοιον implies at least duality, though the satirist
needs some acceptable standards by which he may attack what he
sees around him. Petronius' standards in literature were old-fashioned, classical, and as far as we can see, his contemptuous view of philosophical and rhetorical attitudinizing probably appealed to Tacitus.
There was, quite probably, a Roman-ness in Petronius which cut
through the adventitious layers of philosophy that overlaid Roman
character in the intellectuals of the opposition. Such naturalism as we
find in the *Satyricon* suggests[34] an attempt to illustrate the truth of
human behaviour and the absurdity of human acts, without any great
amount of protreptic zeal for reform, or even a marked degree of protest.
The *Satyricon* has its own integrity of intention as a work of art: beyond this, it is difficult to make sure comment about his personality
on the basis of his work alone – especially in its imperfect state of
survival. We may note, however, his sceptical attitude to human
friendship as it emerges in the poem of ch. 80, which sums up the
continuous process of mutual betrayal that is a salient feature of the
relationships between Encolpius, Ascyltos, Giton – and later Eumolpus.

[32] Suet. *Divus Claudius* 26, 29, 36. Tac. *Annales* XI, 32-2.

[33] Tac. *Annales* XVI, 20, 1-2: *Ambigenti Neroni quonam modo noctium suarum
ingenia notescerent, offertur Silia, matrimonio senatoris haud ignota et ipsa ad
omnem libidinem adscita ac Petronio perquam familiaris. agitur in exilium tamquam
non siluisset quae viderat pertuleratque, proprio odio.*

[34] On the other hand, Sullivan 97-8 admits a strong strain of "realism" (or
'naturalism') in Petronius, but is careful to stress the element of fantasy in the
whole construction, and concedes that P's aim was in no sense to present life as
it was lived.

Petronius' custom of turning night into day may indicate,[35] apart from other things, a withdrawal from contact with other people.

One of the most difficult parts of an attempt to discover what Petronius was like is the elucidation of his attitude to sex. It is true that some of the sexual episodes in his work suggest the attitude of the Epicureans to the whole subject, – but not entirely.[36] Certainly there is an Epicurean absence of warmth in the parts of the *Satyricon* which deal with sexual relationships, (heterosexual or homosexual); even the pyrotechnics of passionate language suggest despair more often than ecstasy, and are very literary.[37] They do not give the impression of being intended for serious consideration any more than the threats of suicide that occur in the work. It may be that the case which J. P. Sullivan has made out to prove that Petronius was scopophile will carry some conviction.[38] This subtle analysis of the sexual themes of the *Satyricon* relies largely upon internal evidence of the text itself, and is based upon an identification between Petronius and Encolpius. Such an identification is not easily established in the sphere of ordinary critical argument, but in the logic of psychoanalytical interpretation it is legitimate enough, and something can be made of it. If we follow Sullivan along these lines, we shall agree, probably with justice, that Petronius was something of a *voyeur*; but we might also ask, what artist is not? The line between abnormal and normal visual curiosity, or susceptibility to fantasy, is not drawn rigidly in our own society. A writer who is frank in his curiosity about sexual relationships, will

---

[35] Tac. *Annales* XVI, 18, 1: *nam illi dies per somnum, nox officiis et oblectamentis vitae transigebatur.*

[36] For the Epicurean attitude to sex: οὐ γὰρ ἔγωγε ἔχω τί νοήσω τἀγαθόν, ἀφαιρῶν μὲν τὰς διὰ χυλῶν ἡδονάς, ἀφαιρῶν δὲ τὰς δι' ἀφροδισίων, ἀφαιρῶν δὲ τὰς δι' ἀκροαμάτων, ἀφαιρῶν δέ καὶ τὰς διὰ μορφῆς κατ' ὄψιν ἡδείας κινήσεις. C. Bailey, *Epicurus, the Extant Remains*, Oxford 1926, 122 (Fragm. 10, Usener 67: from Athenaeus 546 e. and Diog. Laert. X, 6). Bailey's comment (390) on this apparently straightforward acceptance of sex in the περὶ τέλους as an important and legitimate source of human pleasure, suggests that it be read in the light of πρὸς Μενοικεα 129 5–11: καὶ ἐπεὶ πρῶτον ἀγαθὸν τοῦτο καὶ σύμφυτον, διὰ τοῦτο καὶ οὐ πᾶσαν ἡδονὴν αἱρούμεθα, ἀλλ' ἔστιν ὅτε πολλὰς ἡδονὰς ὑπερβαίνομεν, ὅταν πλεῖον ἡμῖν τὸ δυσχερὲς ἐκ τούτων ἔπηται; καὶ πολλὰς ἀλγηδόνας ἡδονῶν κρείττους νομίζομεν, ἐπειδὰν μείζων ἡμῖν ἡδονὴ παρακολουθῇπολὺν χρόνον ὑπομείνασι τὰς ἀλγηδόνας. πᾶσα οὖν ἡδονὴ διὰ τὸ φύσιν ἔχειν οἰκείαν ἀγαθόν, οὐ πᾶσα μέντοι αἱρετή. Cicero used this passage from the περὶ τέλους to suggest as strongly as possible that Epicurean philosophy was positively hedonistic: see Usener *Epicurea* 118–120 on fg. 67. But see Usener fg. 62 (118) συνουσίη ὤνησε μὲν οὐδέποτε, ἀγαπτὸν δὲ εἰ μὴ ἔβλαψε (Diog. L. X, 118).

[37] Especially 80, 3; 94; *cf.* the use of the word *tragoedia* 101, 7; 108, 11; 140, 6.

[38] J. P. Sullivan, "The Satiricon of Petronius, Some Psychoanalytical Considerations." *The American Imago* Vol. 18, 4, 1961, 352-69 recapitulated with

inevitably seem to some people to have an immoderate visual interest in them, and to be unusual, if not abnormal. In Roman society it was not uncommon to have frankly sexual scenes depicted in wall-paintings. It was common enough, though not universally approved.[39] Men of the respectable standing of Horace could have rooms with appropriately disposed mirrors, to provide multifarious images of coitus.[40] In such a context we must place Petronius' alleged scopophilia. In itself, this interest would not appear startling to his contemporaries, but his apparently naturalistic writing about the subject might cause surprise. Ovid's poems about sex and the spirit of these wall paintings are very much of common substance. Petronius would appear to offer something different – somewhat harsher, no less heartless.

No doubt his stress upon impotence, the anger of Priapus, and the fearsome aspect of sexually menacing females strike a note of weirdness, like the image of the "dark woman" that haunted Proust's last days.[41] The Circe episode has an element of hysteria in it that we may recall when we read the "Circe" passage of James Joyce's *Ulysses*,[42] or the frantic self-abasement and fluctuations of emotion of the same writer in some of his early letters to his wife. Whether Petronius had the shape

additions in ch. VIII of his "The Satyricon of Petronius, A Literary Study."

[39] Propertius II 6, 27-34:
> *quae manus obscenas depinxit prima tabellas*
> *et posuit casta turpis uisa domo,*
> *illa puellarum ingenuos corrupit ocellos*
> *nequitiaeque suae noluit esse rudes.*
> *a gemat, in terris ista qui protulit arte*
> *iurgia sub tacita condita laetitia!*
> *non istis olim uariabant tecta figuris:*
> *tum paries nullo crimine pictus erat.*

For examples see: *Herculaneum et Pompeii,Recueil Général des Peintures, Bronzes,* Vol. VIII, *Le Musée Secret,* H. Roux, M. L. Barré, Paris 1872.

[40] Suetonius: *Ad res Venerias intemperantior traditur; nam speculato cubiculo scorta dicitur habuisse disposita, ut quocumque respecisset ibi ei imago coitus referretur.* Ed. C. L. Roth, Teubner. Lips 1882, p. 298. E. Fraenkel, *Horace* Oxford 1957, 21, suggests that this was a *communis locus* of ancient biographies based on *rumores* and compares Seneca on Hostius Quadra *Nat Quaest* 1, 16, 2: or Ps.-Acro on Hor. *Ep.* 1, 19, 1: about Cratinus the Athenian comic dramatist. The evidence of wall-paintings and the like does not suggest that such stories were necessarily untrue.

[41] G. D. Painter, *Marcel Proust, A Biography* Vol. II, London 1965.

[42] *Cf.* the "Circe" or "Night-town" episode in Joyce's *Ulysses* on its somewhat "Petronian" background, see the discussion in R. Ellmann, *James Joyce,* Oxford 1959, 377 ff. Joyce himself exhibits the fluidity of mood of the character in "Circe" (which is reminiscent of the psychological fluidity of Petronius' character) in his letter to his wife from Dublin in 1909, Ellmann 291-7.

of personality that such phenomena might suggest, it is impossible to say. It is perhaps significant that he found comparably fluid personalities worthy of examination and description. It is hard to deny that beneath the stratifications of satire there is a visible seam of sympathy for unhappiness, and that under the picaresque, there is a regard for honesty.

SOME COMMENTS ON PETRONIUS' PORTRAYAL OF CHARACTER

Within the broken economy of the *Satyricon's* remains, Petronius' characters move convincingly. There are few characters in the work that are not drawn with their own special life. The Roman satiric tradition,[1] and the works of the Greek characterologists who were possibly in some rapport with the Athenian New Comedy,[2] provided a copious history and abundant material and models for his character-drawing. Nor must we omit to mention the influence upon him of older classical authors.[3] Part of the standard rhetorical education was concerned with the bundles of qualities that represented recurrent personality types.[4] Petronius took this material, which he thought was inadequate in itself and rather jaded,[5] and added to it his own digested observations of life, forming a blend of unprecedented originality in Roman letters. Life as well as literature produced his charac-

---

[1] J. P. Sullivan takes the view that the *Satyricon* rather than being a *Kreuzung der Gattungen* is a natural development within the boundaries of Menippean satire: *The Satyricon of Petronius* London 1968, 115, *cf.* 89; C. A. Van Rooy, *Studies in Classical Satire and Related Literary Theory*, Leiden 1965, 154–5. But *cf.* W. Kroll, *Studien zum Verständnis der Römischen Literatur*, Darmstadt 1959, 223–4 "Die Kreuzung der Gattungen."

[2] Theophrastus' Χαρακτῆρες (*cf.* also Aristotle *Rhet* II ch. 12–17: Ariston of Ceos, Aratos, and Philodemos the Epicurean philosopher of the First Century B. C. wrote characterologies: see Schmid-Stählin, *Geschichte der Griechischen Literatur* II, 1. 64. The view that Menander had been a pupil of Theophrastus is best treated with caution: A. Lesky, *History of Greek Literature* (transl. Willis, De Heer) London 1966, 644–5. O. Raith emphasises the resemblance between P's description of character and Philodemus περὶ κακιῶν (and Theophrastus): *Petronius ein Epicuroor*. Diss. Erlangen 1963, 20–3.

[3] Sullivan 165, 167.

[4] S. F. Bonner, *Roman Declamation in the Late Republic and Early Empire*, California 1949, 160–1.

[5] *Satyricon* 1. 1–3.

terisation, and it is probably its contact with life which gives it its greatest measure of vigour[6].

This aspect of Petronius' genius has produced some of the most fascinating human material in Roman literature. It is a pity that some of the ablest Petronian criticism of recent decades has emphasised so much the limitations placed upon his character-drawing power by the literary forms of his age.[7] I hope to suggest that many of the reservations expressed in such criticisms, are unnecessarily restrictive. Apart from the most prominent personae, characters in general in the *Satyricon* appear and disappear rapidly, almost as if they were flashed on to a screen.[8] They are presented with what seems to be great economy, though the cinematic impression is enhanced by the broken nature of our text. Little enough is said in narrative: they are allowed, for a considerable part, to reveal themselves by means of their own words,[9] which need not be plentiful, but are usually pregnant. Even minor characters have a sufficient depth of dimension to suggest that they have lives to lead outside the boundaries of the text.[10] In the case of the principal characters, of whom we have more particular information, we are aware that only a portion is visible above the surface. Conscious or unconscious motives are adumbrated, which may provide a basis for psychoanalytical interpretation.[11] However, the more apparently self-revealing are the words uttered by these characters, the more difficult it is to fathom their natures. They share this measure of opacity with their creator, Petronius.[12] It will be recalled also how difficult it is to estimate the personality and motives of Ovid, who, even when he is at his most apparently self-revealing, seems to keep back the essence of his personality.

Just as Petronius could penetrate other people's characters, we may infer from Tacitus' biography of him that he could analyse his own personality.[13] His insight is clearly revealed even in those minor

[6] Which Sullivan does not regard as naturalistic in the modern sense: 97; E. Auerbach, *Mimesis*, transl. Trask, Princeton 1953, 28–33.

[7] Sullivan, 97, 101, 104: "the work is not so much a depiction of the real, for our moral instruction, as a denigration of the real." See also refs. at note 6 above.

[8] *Cf.* E. Dujardin, *Le Monologue Intérieur*, Paris 1931, 47–8.

[9] Sullivan 59, 69, 82; R. Hirzel, *Der Dialog*, Lips 1895, II 37.

[10] 30, 6–11; 70, 13.

[11] Sullivan, ch. VII 232–253; which is a modification of his paper "The *Satyricon* of Petronius, some Psychoanalytical Considerations," *American Imago* Vol. 18, 1961, 325–369: he argues that Petronius had scopophilic tendencies.

[12] See Tacitus' account of his personality: *Annales* XVI, 17–20.

[13] The expressions in Tacitus' biography: *ac dicta factaque eius quanto solutiora et quandam sui neglegentiam praeferentia, tanto gratius in speciem sim-*

characters who have their brief say at Trimalchio's dinner-party.[14]
They are self-deceptive and yet strangely innocent boasters in their
pretence that they are not merely parasites of one of their own kind
who has had astonishing success. Their aggressiveness reveals a latent
sense of their own lowly position,[15] which is indicated also by the
crudeness of their speech and style.[16] This aggressiveness is an imitation of Trimalchio's superb arrogance which itself is a metamorph
of his original lowness. Later in the work (112), Lichas, the ship-
owner, shows anger at the widow of Ephesus, whose story is told,[17]
because he compares her defections with those of his own wife - a snap
identification that occurs in his irritated and irrational mind. These are
examples of the angles from which Petronius chooses to view his parti-
cipants in the human tragi-farce. Certain female figures, such as
Quartilla, Tryphaena, and the widow of Croton, are sinister and sexually menacing, as well as being ridiculous. Oenothea and Proselenus are
lower counterparts of Quartilla.[18] The principal three characters,
Encolpius, Ascyltos and Giton, are markedly unstable, and are, like
the characters of mime,[19] essentially "on the run,"[20] pursued by the

plicitatis accipiebantur. (Annales XVI, 18,2) and: neque tamen praeceps vitam
expulit, sed incisas venas, ut libitum, obligatas aperire rursum et adloqui amicos,
non per seria aut quibus gloriam constantiae peteret. audiebatque referentis nihil
de immortalitate animae et sapientium placitis, sed levia carmina et facilis versus.
(19, 2) suggest a certain capacity for self-examination.

[14] 41,9; 46; Frank Frost Abbott, "The Use of language as a means of Characterisation in Petronius," Classical Philology 2, 43–50. On the style of the more
sophisticated characters: Peter George's article "Style and Character in the
Satyricon: Arion Vol. V, 3, 336–358 analyses the literary elements in their talk.

[15] Perhaps they were agents of his: H. C. Schnur, "The Economic Background
of the Satyricon," Latomus, 18, 1959, 790–9, 792.

[16] Abbott, 43–4.

[17] 41,9; 113, 2–4: at non Lichas risit, sed iratum
commovens caput " si iustus" inquit "imperator fuisset, debuit patris familiae
corpus in monumentum referre, mulierem affigere cruci". non dubie redierat
in animum Hedyle expilatumque libidinosa migratione navigium. sed nec foederis
verba permittebant meminisse, nec hilaritas, quae occupaverat mentes, dabat iracundiae locum: Assuming that Hedyle is his wife.

[18] Also the un-named girl accompanying the peasants: 14, 5 mulier operto
capite, quae cum rustico steterat, who, if 16, 3 (illa scilicet quae paulo ante cum
rustico steterat) is accepted as genuine, may be the maid of Quartilla. On this
question, Sullivan 46–7, Nisbet's review of Konrad Müller's text Journal of
Roman Studies 1962, 227–8.

[19] The Mimes of Herodas by W. Headlam, A. D. Knox, Cambridge 1966, Introduction esp. xxii–xxiii.

[20] For this comical "chase" associated with the mime: Cicero Pro Caelio 65:
Mimi ergo iam exitus, non fabulae; in quo cum clausula non invenitur, fugit aliquis e
manibus, dein scabilla concrepant, aulaeum tollitur: see R. G. Austin's comment
ad. loc. M. Tulli Ciceronis, Pro Marco Caelio Oratio, Oxford 1952.

intractability of the world and the inevitability of debasing misfortunes: they have no policy and in no respect are they in control of their actions. Trimalchio and his friends, however, are a circle of people who exhibit a credible, vivid, but also farcical social pattern consisting of satellites around a rich man who wishes to assume that everybody and everything orbits about him.

None of these are merely "types," though it would be possible to refer them in a general way to the human typology of the Satire, Mime, New Comedy, which was influenced by the "characterology" of Fourth Century philosophers such as Plato,[21] Aristotle,[22] Theophrastus.[23] Typology in a sense goes back to the sophists;[24] Plato produced his own array of human types in the *Republic*, which probably was influenced by Sicilian mime.[25] Aristotle's presentation of character is incidental to his philosophy, but Theophrastus presented specimens of the human personality with the meticulous care of an artist. Characterology thus stood with one foot in the philosopher's lecture hall, and the other in the kitchen of the Menippean satire. Its rhetorical and philosophical associations rigidified in the typical Greek novel, where characters are allowed to possess very few idiosyncrasies,[26] and move along almost entirely predictable lines. This sterility is probably parodied by Petronius, along with that of other literary genres; he stigmatises especially the contemporary rhetorical education, as rigid and inane. The base from which he mounts his attack is an appreciation and knowledge of the older classical authors. The epic in particular influences his ap-

---

[21] *Rep.* 548 d. *Gorg.* 493 d, his ἠθοποιία: R. G. Ussher's comments, *The Characters of Theophrastus* Intro. 27; For Plato's description of the "timocratic" man: *Rep.* 549 d ff; the "democratic" man: 559 d ff., the "tyrannical" man: 571 a ff. H. Reich, *Der Mimus*, Berlin 1903 Bd. II, 355, 360, 363.

[22] On resemblances between Theophrastus' Χαρακτῆρες and Aristotle, Ussher, 8–11, who is careful to stress the difference in style and time of Theophrastus' work from those of his master (at *Rhet.* 9, 26; III, 7. 6, for example). Also E. Schwartz, *Ethik der Griechen* edit. Richter, Stuttgart 1951, 16 f.

[23] Characterology as such first emerges in its full form with Theophrastus' Χαρακτῆρες, Schmid-Stählin, II, 1. 64. Ussher does not agree with the view that this work has a direct ethical purpose, and suggests that it might have been intended to serve for a *Poetic*.

[24] If we accept that Thucydides' descriptions of the character of peoples (as in Thuc. I, 70) or individuals (Pericles: Thuc. II, 65) or the so-called Melian Dialogue (Thuc. V, 84–114) are (a) sufficiently in the manner of ἠθοποιία (b) are sophistic and dialogue: R. Hirzel, *Der Dialog* I, 45, 53; Protagoras was said to be the inventor of the "Socratic" dialogue Diog. 9, 53 (Hirzel 56).

[25] Reich, *op. cit.*

[26] F. A. Todd, *Some Ancient Novels*, Oxford 1940, 80.

proach to decadent contemporary practices. His satirical mimesis is directed against such writers as Publilius Syrus and Lucan.[27] Knowledge of the older classics provides Petronius with the necessary field of reference outside his own time and place, and he has in this antiquity a measure, mainly literary, but not exclusive of ethical implication,[28] which he can place against the debauchery and slackness, both moral and literary, of those with whom he has to live. He is not a *laudator temporis acti* of the same bitter stamp as Aristophanes, or even of the same kind as his own minor characters, one of whom (44) bemoans (a human touch) at once the decay of religion and the high price of bread.[29] He has sympathy, and he is more tolerant of the foibles of his contemporaries than he appears to be at first glance. Quite simply, he seems to have a range of awareness of literature that is very wide, surpassing all but a few of the intellectuals of his time.[30] This extends far beyond the common limits of an age of stale rhetoric and inferior popular song. As Menippus[31], and as Petronius' own predecessors in Roman satire[32] attempted to improve and criticise standards of social custom, so Petronius attempted in the cultural sphere to suggest standards of taste, which were not merely classical, or archaic, but were intended to be reasonable.[33]

[27] Sullivan 67, 168–9, 191–2; H. Stubbe, "Die Verseinlagen im Petron," *Philologus Supplement* bd. XXV Hefte, 1933 (esp. 103) argues that stylistically, the *Bellum Civile* poem is Vergilian rather than imitative of Lucan's style, and an implied criticism of L. on stylistic as well as other grounds. *cf.* K. F. C. Rose, "Problems of Chronology in Lucan's career," *T. A. P. A.* Vol. XCVII, 1966, 379–396.

[28] Sullivan, 259: "If there is a 'quasi-moral' principle at work, it is the principle, invoked sometimes by Horace also, of taste, be it taste in literature or behaviour; but taste itself dictates that even this be not taken too seriously" *surtout pas de zèle: cf.* J. F. Killeen on Petronius, "James Joyce's Roman Prototype," *Comparative Literature* IX, 3, 1957, 193–203, rejects alike (201) the tendency to see ethically significant implications and intentions in the *Satyricon* (Burman, Klebs and others) and in *Ulysses*.

[29] 44. 2, 3, 17, 18; Schnur, *op. cit.;* P. A. Brunt, "The Roman Mob," *Past and Present*, 35, 1966, 3–27.

[30] A. Rini, *Petronius in Italy*, N. Y. 1957. 159. E. Courtney, "Parody and Literary allusion in Menippean Satire," *Philologus* 102, 1/2, 1962, 86–100.

[31] E. Zeller, *Philosophie der Griechen* II i. (ed. 5 Darmstadt 1963) 286 7; E. Rohde, *Der Griechische Roman*, Hildesheim 1960, 267.

[32] Note above 28; Varros' work sometimes had a distinct political purpose, e.g. τριχάρανος, Hirzel I, 455.

[33] Sullivan, 89; G. M. A. Grube, *The Greek and Roman Critics*, London 1965, 196–8; L. P. Wilkinson, "Philodemus and Poetry", *Greece and Rome* 2. 1933, 144 ff.

Before we come to discuss the individual characters, we may consider an important submerged entity in the work. It is not the author's own personality; though this is of importance in the *Satyricon*, and is inevitably revealed in it and by it. It is the society itself of the First Century B. C. which is the most striking implicit "character" in the *Satyricon*. This age was the mother of Petronius and all his characters, and also of Nero and Seneca and Tigellinus. It was an age of great economic growth in the shadow of a principate which had struck root, and it produced patches of prosperity[34] from which a number of individuals benefited to a vast degree. Secure communications, the absence of serious civil war, a centralised administration composed of new men, *equites*, or freedmen – all were factors which contributed towards the increase in prosperity. Archaeological evidence from the remains of trading cities such as Ostia, is itself sufficient testimony to the movement of these times.[35] They wanted cultural anchorage, and to be admired as great patrons. They lacked judgment, but they were eager. Education was spread thinner to meet the new demand.[36] The arts adopted self-conscious and extreme forms in order to meet this demand which always sought to purchase something new and original.[37] Many of the restraints of ancient *religio* were dissolved, but the new men were more superstitious than the Republican oligarchy.[38] Philosophy

[34] On the relative smallness of Trimalchio's fortune, Sullivan, 150.

[35] Schnur, 791; Russell Meiggs, *Roman Ostia*, Oxford 1960, 70.

[36] Meiggs, 222–3.

[37] Petronius ridicules artistic extremes in his parodies, but it may be recalled that in fact, at a celebration of games given by Nero, *inter pyrricharum argumenta taurus Pasiphaaen ligneo invencae simulacro abditam iniit, ut multi spectantium crediderunt* (Suet, *Nero* 12) *cf.* 21: *inter cetera cantavit Canacen parturientem Oresten matricidam etc.*

[38] *cf.* the story of the *versipellis*, 62, also its echo 63, and the resultant superstitious dread on the part of Trimalchio's guests in 64. The Roman senatorial "establishment" at least endeavoured to control the introduction of new magico-religious ideas into the city: A. Toynbee, *Hannibal's Legacy*, Oxford 1965, Vol. II, 400 f, 912 f; Augustus caused a large number of the Sibylline oracles to be destroyed in 12 B. C. on the grounds that: *nullis vel parum idoneis auctoribus ferebatur*, whereas he preserved the genuine ones (Suet. *Aug* 31. 1.). On this question see G. W. Clarke "The Burning of Books and Catullus 36", *Latomus* XXVII, 515 ff. The attitude of the Republican ruling class to magic and the like was essentially social – they feared that it might subvert society, indeed the attitude that underlay the S. C. *de Bacchanalibus*, 186 B.C. is strikingly persistent in Tacitus' stigmatisation of Christianity as an *exitiabilis superstitio* (*Annales* XV, 44, 4). Though the magic dreads of Trimalchio and his friends may be native Italian in origin and thus not eligible for suppression and severe reprobation, few respectable persons of the Republic would have admitted them, and n Imperial times, adherents of the Republican style like Tacitus, would have despised them. Servilia gave money to *magi* to see if her father Soranus would

was represented on as many levels of respectability as the worship of the gods. The so-called "Stoic Opposition" of those who opposed the principate in eager retrospect for the Republic's *libertas* were strongly influenced by philosophical ideas.[39] On lower levels of social and political endeavour, the philosophical basis for life was supplied by Cynic streetcorner preachers.[40]

The advent of the new rich had broken the continuity with the past almost as effectively as the civil conflict had decimated the senatorial aristocracy, and ended the hope of the old Republic's restoration. Society held the possibility of an exciting and rewarding career even for the humblest person, though not for many of such. In this society, a poor boy, even if he were an ex-slave from an Eastern province of the empire, could possibly end as a millionaire and enjoy not only the power conferred by his wealth, but a new status.[41] It was easy for Greek or Hellenised intellectuals to make a living from the nascent cultural tastes of such men.[42] A society of wandering philosophers ranged the country like goliardic singers, or like Jack Kerouac's characters in *On the Road*. Society easily tolerated the light burden which they represented. But at the same time this was an age which was heartbreaking to its more refined spirits.[43] The intellectuals' attitude to such a society of the rich was often *odi et amo*, and in the case of some of the less fortunate, this was speedily reduced to *odi*. The attitudes that emanated from affluence and the decreasingly less critical attitudes to materialist values depressed the intellectuals of First Century AD Italy, just as Plato was depressed by Syracuse.[44] The *Satyricon* reveals the dilemma of the intellectual who is torn between his desire to partici-

be spared, which is made a charge against her in her trial together with her father (Tac. *Annales* XVI, 30, 2; 31, 1)

[39] Stoics could hardly be expected to feel much sympathy with the pretensions of a princeps who allowed himself to be worshipped as a god, as emerges in the reign of Gaius, E. V. Arnold, *Roman Stoicism*, London 1911, 393, and on the "Old Roman" – Stoic opposition to Nero, 394–9; B. W. Henderson, *The Life and Principate of the Emperor Nero*, London 1903, 294–302, also ch. XI *passim*.

[40] There was some of this plain outspokenness even in such respectable figures as Demetrius the Cynic, the friend of Thrasea: Dio Cassius 66, 11, 13; Suet Vesp. 13. See also H. Musurillo, *Acts of the Pagan Martyrs*, Oxford 1954.

[41] 75, 10 – 77, 7.

[42] A. H. Salonius: "Die Griechen und das Griechische in Petrons Cena Trimalchionis", *Societas Scientiarum Fennica, Commentationes Humanarum Litterarum*, Helsingfors 1927, II i, 15.

[43] Even under an earlier and more humane dispensation, Horace had been able to withdraw from too close an association with the *princeps*, Suet. *Vita Horati* 25, C. L. Roth.

[44] Plato *Ep.* VII 326 b, c.

pate in an exciting prosperity, and his awareness of the thinness of
the cultural superficies upon which his patrons oblige him to perform.
Petronius expresses his difficulties in one mode; later on, Tacitus, who
had clearly some sympathy for Petronius' predicament, [45] expresses
his hatred of the frustrating times in another. Tacitus had the advantage of surviving to write in a period when the empire had its opportu-
nity to draw breath after its first prolonged attack of horrors.[46]
Tacitus was a man of archaic strictness and integrity.[47] Even more
frustrated was Juvenal, expressing his common-sense Roman animus
against a society which profited intellectual frauds and let men of
worth subsist on pittances.[48]

But Petronius had the deepest comprehension of the discontents of
Imperial society. He could empathise the experiences of the depressed
and disaffiliated. He was less stiffened by *gravitas* than Tacitus, and
not so thwarted as Juvenal. He floated with the stream for a long time,
though he was at last immersed. He was jocular rather than jaundiced
in his writing, and the statement which his work in general enunciates,
is a calm one, no matter how irrational or hysterical are some of its
components.[49] Notwithstanding this, he is doomed, and he knows it.
His characters from time to time express hysterical despair, and then
are switched away from it. Is this his own despair? Did he cultivate a
volatility which could turn it aside for a period? If we hypothesise a
literary receptacle for such despair, perhaps we might suggest that
Encolpius, who narrates the novel as we have it, plays the author's
part. Possibly this Encolpius is Petronius, as Petronius might have been
if he had been unsuccessful. The onus of proof, however, still lies with
those who would go so far as Conrad Cichorius who suggests that there
are indications of a connection between Petronius and the city of
Massilia from which Encolpius may have fled as scapegoat.[50] Massi-

---

[45] This is indicated by the amount of interest shown by Tacitus in the life
history of P. *cf.* H. D. Rankin, "On Tacitus' Biography of Petronius," *Classica
et Mediaevalia* XXVI, 1–2 1965, 233–45; (see below, 106–108).

[46] Tacitus, *Histories* I, 1.

[47] R. Syme, *Tacitus*, Oxford 1958, 553.

[48] Juvenal III 147–53, VII 66 ff.
G. Highet, *Juvenal the Satirist*, Oxford 1959, 7–19.

[49] A statement of what B. E. Perry, *The Ancient Romances, A Literary-
Historical Account of their Origins*, California 1967, calls his "profound but latent
pessimism." This coolness is characteristic of Epicurean literary doctrine:
Sullivan 57; Grube, 195–6; Wilkinson 146, 149–50; Philodemus *Über Die Gedichte*,
C. Jensen, Berlin 1923, II, 21 – III 5 (ff. 11,13).

[50] C. Cichorius, "Petronius und Massilia," *Römische Studien* Berlin 1922,
138–9.

liote connections, even if they are established in the case both of the author and his creation, are not conclusive evidence for the author's life-history, but the fact that the story (at least in the surviving portion) is in Encolpius' hands, counts for something. He is the mouthpiece for the intellectual discontents of the age, and his sexual impotence itself might be taken as a symbol of the age's intellectual futility. The symbolism may or may not be there, but if it is, it may even have been unconsciously implanted by this most selfconscious author. The theme of impotence is appropriate. The intellectual, in spite of Seneca and others, was powerless. The First Century A. D. was not the age of Petronius, or even of Gaius and Nero; it was in an important sense, the age of Trimalchio.

Where, within the bounds of antiquity or modernity, could one find a time more appropriate to a disillusioned wanderer like Encolpius than the age of which he is a product? Encolpius is a displaced and anomic man. He is an Odysseus for whom there is no known destination, and no homecoming of which we are aware.[51] Encolpius is carried off helpless by the tide of First Century society; he is certainly less able than Petronius to keep his footing against it. Nevertheless, Encolpius can, to some extent, discriminate the experience that flows over him. He has a high intelligence which has been sharpened by a good education. But he does not discriminate to any purpose. He allows his emotions to bear him off, and surrenders to their power in no romantic sense, but because he sees no sufficient reason to do anything else. He moves rapidly from the pole of hysterical misery and near suicide to that of extreme hilarity and unfounded optimism.[52] He has rejected conventional civilisation apart from the margin that gives him subsistence, and even this he does not positively accept.[53] He is a casual predator and occasional parasite. Even in his suicidal moments,[54] he must live, and so he must remain in some relation with his environment. Somewhere or somehow, perhaps even from the beginning, he lost the centripetal forces of conscience or reflection, and he gives the impression of a personality which has no persistent inner core, but is composed

---

[51] Such as the final reconciliation with life in Apuleius' *Metamorphoses*.

[52] For examples of his instability, 16–25; 80, 7; 82, 4.

[53] As in the case of the "beats" so it might be said of P's character that: "the pursuit of long-range goods is abandoned for the pleasures and the anguish of the moment." Elwin H. Powell in Arnold H. Rose, *Human Behavior and Social Process, An Interactionist Approach, London 1962, 361*.

[54] 80, 7.

of waves of anxiety.[55] He has moved back from the "guilt culture" to the "shame culture," and he is swiftly leaving the ambience of the "shame culture" also in his retrogressive journey.[56] His personality has something of the shape of that of a Homeric hero[57] debased and chronologically displaced. He is mutable, unreflectingly egoistic, and seems to be capable of unlimited variability of attitudes which are not linked by any common element other than his capacity to react swiftly towards immediate or short term pleasure stimuli.[58]

Encolpius' "interior monologue" does not entail a Socratic observation of self so much as the egotistic objectivity of a Homeric hero describing what is happening within him, but with almost indulgent objectivity refraining from moral judgment on himself. Such a personality freely admits discreditable motives and calmly discusses their ineluctable influence upon his attitude and action. Homeric man is thought to be concerned with the circumstances of outward honour, and is not shameless. But no mark or public ridicule diverts Encolpius from his ways for more than a short time: Encolpius does not care.

To pursue the Homeric analogy a little further, we might argue that the difference between the Homeric and Petronian casts of personality was essentially this: the Homeric characters, if we follow (though at some distance) the Dodds/Snell view of their problem, were preconscientious, whereas the people we encounter in Petronius' narrative are postconscientious. The former belong to a time when conscientious self-control was not generally a condition of remaining a member of human society: the latter to a time when changing views about society and art allowed the long outmoded fluid, primitivistic shape of personality to be a possible object of artistic attention once more. This analogy is hardly affected, whether we regard "Homer" as more concerned with depicting a primitive age, or as treating a decadent one in a romantically primitivising style. On the other hand, Homeric influence in Petronius has been sufficiently striking to cause Klebs and many others to see a Homeric parody in his work. The Greek novel had Homeric associations, particularly with the *Odyssey*,[59] and Klebs'

55 *Cf.* J. P. Donleavy's "Sebastian Dangerfield" in *The Ginger Man*, or (a most extreme example of antiheroism) Keith Waterhouse's *Jubb*.

56 E. R. Dodds, *The Greeks and the Irrational*, California 1951, 17 ff.

57 Dodds, *op. cit.* in his chapter "Agamemnon's Apology" *passim*.

58 *Cf.* G. S. Kirk, *Homer and the Epic*, Cambridge 1965, 101–2, on the "monumental" aspect of Homer's work exemplified in his use of pre-existing material.

59 A theme drawn into Hellenistic literature and into the novel via the later tragedy: E. Rohde, *Der Griechische Roman und seine Vorläufer*, Hildesheim 1960, 110, 111.

position was that Encolpius is a species of dishonourable Odysseus, pursued by the wrath of Priapus, as his illustrious predecessor was by the relentless anger of Poseidon.[60] There is a long tradition of parody connected with the Odyssey and the view that a novel which contains some specific Homeric parodies is itself a Homeric parody, remains attractive.[61] If we equate Encolpius with Odysseus, however approximately, we are faced with a pathetic and absurd "Odysseus" which perhaps is reminiscent of that in the Cynic tradition.[62] He is a wanderer with no home to go to, and no Penelope, faithful or otherwise, awaits his return.[63] How he ended in the full text of the novel, it is impossible to say. Perhaps, after all, a home was found for the wanderer – as happens to Lucius in the *Metamorphoses* of Apuleius, but considering the nature of the *Satyricon*, it is hard to imagine a serious ending, unless perhaps, as itself a final joke on the part of the author. The Odyssean homecoming is, however, paralleled by the reunion of parted lovers in the Hellenistic novel's tradition, and it is possible that Petronius ended his work with some brutal jest along these lines, involving Giton and Encolpius. His brand of realism would hardly allow any end to the wanderings that was free either from tragedy or farce. We cannot exclude the Odyssean analogy, whether we think it comes direct or by means of the Hellenistic romances. Though the text of the *Satyricon* is much broken, the cause and effect of divine wrath is easily enough seen. The origin of his bad luck may occur in the part of the novel that is lost. We are not informed what his transgression was, but clearly it was grossly offensive to Priapus.[64] In fact, Encolpius consistently commits acts which offend the gods. He manages (somewhat unnecessarily) to slaughter a sacred goose of Priapus,[65] which depresses his credit even further with the deity – and this incident reminds us of Odysseus' men killing the oxen of the Sun. A striking effect of his sin is that he is plagued by impotence.[66] His would-be mistress, Chrysis, expresses the opinion that Encol-

---

[60] E. Klebs, "Zur Composition von Petronius' Satirae," *Philologus* 47, 1889, 623–635.

[61] Courtney, *op. cit.*

[62] R. Hoïstad, *Cynic Hero and Cynic King*, Uppsala 1948: and (without prejudice to the question whether or not Antisthenes is classifiable as a proto-cynic), Mullach, Frag. Antist. 25, 26, 27, (ὁμηρικά of Antisthenes) deal with Odysseus.

[63] A conjecture which (I suggest) is not unreasonable in itself but the probability of which is inevitably subject to the incomplete nature of the text which we possess.

[64] Klebs, *op. cit.*; Cichorius, *op. cit.*; Sullivan, 40 ff.

[65] 136, 5–6.

[66] 128, 2, 8–9; 129, 5–7; 133, 3; 134; 139, 4 (probably); 140, 11.

pius' fixation on Giton is the cause of his impotence, but this naturalistic explanation need not detract from the general probability of the
divine curse upon him.[67] At all events, until almost the end, incidents
of apparent good fortune in sexual matters turn out badly for him.[68]

Encolpius' name itself suggests sensuality and Hellenic origins.[69]
Others also in the *Satyricon* have Greek names: Ascyltos for example
and Giton, Encolpius' two principal companions, also Eumolpus.
Agamemnon and Menelaus are minor characters, rhetoricians whose
too Homeric names in themselves represent a satire upon their profession. These Greeks or Hellenised Italiotes, are probably of good
education, but this is not necessarily true of Giton whose name is a
a typical slave name and need not, Greek though it is, suggest an Hellenic origin. He is somewhat more vulgar than his two associates, certainly more than Encolpius, and of these two, Ascyltos seems to be
rather more coarse and insensitive than Encolpius. Ascyltos' name in
itself suggests something of a bravo.[70] His sexual prowess is as notable
as his selfishness, and he has great physical strength. Encolpius is
hardly his inferior in respect of selfishness, but he lacks the unthinking
aggressiveness of his friend. Ascyltos' potency is in sharp contrast with
the inhibitions that torment Encolpius. He is more violent than Encolpius, and has about him something of the aura of a gladiatorial tough
and criminal bar-fly.[71] His attitude to Encolpius alternates between
predatory friendship and cool treachery. The bone of contention between them is again and again the boy Giton and his sexual attractions.
In some respects Ascyltos can be seen as a coarser, hostile shadow of
Encolpius. We get the impression, however, that Encolpius would
wish to be as aggressive himself, if he had the courage and the opportu-
nity.[72] There is no real friendship, no *amicitia* between these two.

---

[67] 128, 8–9.

[68] R. Heinze, "Petron und der Griechische Roman," *Hermes* XXXIV 1899,
494–519, esp. 498.

[69] Salonius, 6: "auf dem Schoss Sitzenden." The name does occur in inscriptions etc. H. Stephanus, *Thesaurus L. Gr.* s.v.; Pape, *Griechische Eigennamen.*

[70] Salonius 6: it means "undisturbed, untouched," ἄσκυλτος Steph.

[71] Notice his extreme aggressiveness and brutalised physique and mentality,
80; 92, 2: there is something "gladiatoral" perhaps about Encolpius' past: see
9, 9; 81, 3; 130, 20. In 80 we have the distinct impression of an inexpert gladiatorial combat between E. and A. See Burmann's comments *ad loc*, and the note
of Gonsalius de Salas (in the Burmann edition).

[72] 82, 1–3: *haec locutus gladio latus cingor, et ne infirmitas militiam perderet,
largioribus cibis excito vires. mox in publicum prosilio furentisque more omnes
circumeo porticus. sed dum attonito vultu efferatoque (animo) nihil aliud quam*

Indeed, the tenor of the novel implies an attack upon the concept of friendship. In ch. 80 there is a bitter little poem about the fallibility and unreliability of friends, which is almost as pessimistic as any Shakespearean locus on the subject.[73]

The boy Giton is the catalyst of trouble between these two characters, and he is the third point of the persistent triangle of relationships. He is a species of "femme fatale" and he sees himself as a source of quarrelling who separates the two friends and reunites them (for more trouble) according to his whim or convenience.[74] He applies moral blackmail, by threatening to kill himself or offering himself to be killed, when rows which he has engineered flare up more fiercely than is suitable to his purpose of playing off one of the friends against the other.[75] Like other suicide threats [76] and attempts in the *Satyricon*, Giton's promises of self-destruction are not to be taken seriously. This suggests as much as anything else, a general sense of the devaluation of life. These wanderers do not care for life sufficiently to succeed in killing themselves, or even to be serious in intending to do so. It requires a Stoic or Cynic conviction to do that. They are simply the victims of outbursts of anomic despair which soon pass, so that they can revert to their old habits once more. The physically weaker members of this triad, Encolpius and Giton, are more hysterical than the more elementary Ascyltos.[77] Later in the *Satyricon*, when Ascyltos has been replaced by Eumolpus, Giton's manoeuvres in playing off Eumolpus against Encolpius are conducted with much greater finesse, and with less violent results. Even though he is a fraud in everything but his bad habits and love of dubious poetry, Eumolpus is not a violent personality. Like any other professional rhetorician or poet in the context of the *Satyricon*, he lives off his capacity to dupe the public and is perfectly

---

caedem et sanguinem cogito frequentiusque manum ad capulum, quem devoveram, refero, notavit me miles, sive ille planus fuit sive nocturnus grassator, et "quid tu" inquit "commilito ex qua legione es aut cuius centuria?"

[73] 80, 9:
  nomen amicitiae sic, quatenus expedit, haeret;
  calculus in tabula mobile ducit opus.
  cum fortuna manet, vultum servatis, amici;
  cum cecidit, turpi vertitis ora fuga.

[74] He comes between them when they are about to fight, announces that he is the cause of dissension, offers himself to be killed, 80, 4: he quite unexpectedly (from Encolpius' point of view) elects to go off with Ascyltos. Later (91, 8) he admits: *cum duos armatos viderem, ad fortiorem confugi.*

[75] 80, 4; 94, 15; 101, 7; 108, 11.

[76] 30, 7; 94, 8; 97, 9; 101, 2; 108, 10–11; 132.

[77] 92, 7–11.

contented with his way of life. He cannot be prevented, in fact, from
exhibiting his art.[78] This is true also of Agamemnon and his satellite
Menelaus. However, to return to Giton: there is no doubt that he pos-
sesses a cynical self-centredness and bland insolence which might ensure his survival and perhaps even make his fortune. This was an age
in which ex-slaves could become rich and powerful. Giton, it turns out,
is a slave; though he is a runaway, he pretends, for purposes of social
convenience, to be the slave of Encolpius[79] and Ascyltos. It is just possible that Giton might develop into a magnate of similar type to Trimalchio, but it may be that Giton does not show the same shrewdness
as Trimalchio in the choice of those to whom he prostitutes himself,[80]
and this, together with his irrationality, may prescribe limits to his
future success. Nevertheless, if he should fall into the right hands, he
could be imagined as prosperous and powerful.

Trimalchio is an excellently realised character: not simply because
we have so much more continuous text about him than about other
individuals. It is a question of character itself. Trimalchio and his
friends have a more positive view of the world, are concerned in action,
and lacking any kind of introspection, develop some amazing foibles
which remind the reader quite strongly of Dickens' characters. Trimalchio is a contrast to Encolpius and Ascyltos, who are buffeted about
by circumstances which they make no consistent attempt to resist.
Trimalchio's thoughtless dynamism and pomposity are thrown into
relief by the "beatnik" passivity of these two, and of the other intellectuals, such as Agamemnon. Some of the minor figures surrounding
Trimalchio, in that they are obviously hangers-on and parasites, approach the irregularity of life of Encolpius and his friends, but Trimalchio himself sets a standard of a successful career that outshines anything else of the kind that there is in the book as we have it. Credit
is surely due to a person who was a slave in his youth, was a foreigner
in Italy,[81] and suffered the serious reverses of his early business career.

[78] Even at the risk of a stoning, 90, 1 or a beating, 92, 6.

[79] The reference to him as a *gladiator* 9, 9, might suggest slave status: Tryphaena's remark, 105, 11: *meruisse quidem contumeliam aliquam fugitivos, quibus
in odium bona sua venissent*, might also suggest this; it is possible that the plurals
simply refer to Giton.

[80] 75, 11.

[81] Trimalchio is not Roman: *tam magnus ex Asia veni quam hic candelabrus
est*: 75, 10: on the question of the Semitic name: *Trimalchio* see L. Friedländer's
note on 26, *Petronii Cena Trimalchionis*, Amsterdam 1960, 209; W. D. Lowe,
Petronii Cena Trimalchionis, Cambridge 1905, 3. Salonius, 6; Meiggs, 224:
"Malchio, Malchus" etc.

Against his ignorance and vulgarity, faults, by the way, which have been somewhat overstressed by critics,[82] there is set his immense energy and psychological resilience. It was no small achievement, having been sold into slavery in a foreign country, to gain freedom and a fortune.[83] Like other young slaves, Trimalchio was used as a sexual object by his master and later by his mistress.[84] So far from being broken in spirit by this (or rendered touchy and unbalanced like Giton), Trimalchio set to work to maximise the advantages that could come to him from this situation. Eventually, he ceases to be the utensil, and becomes the user, for he so prevails upon the affections of his master that he obtains manumission and inherits money from him. This change from the slave situation is probably a more frequent version and a more plausible one of the Stoic paradox that only a slave is really a king.[85] Trimalchio went into a trading venture with his inheritance and when the ships laden with his merchandise came to grief, he found himself in a very difficult position. However, he liquified whatever property he had, and his wife sold her jewellery, so that he could remain solvent and try once more. This time the voyage in which he invested turned out to be a prosperous one, and he began to be rich. He then took to the more profitable and secure occupation of financing freedmen like himself.[86] No doubt the freedmen who are present at his dinner-party are in his debt.

The gloomy prognostications about the economic state of Italy that are uttered by some of the minor characters at the *Cena* may be true, for ancient prosperity was patchy, but they also indicate their own relative lack of success in the game which Trimalchio has played with genius(44). The period was a prosperous one, and social advances and social mobility were remarkable in it. Trimalchio's rise in status was phenomenal even for this time. In Ostia, a prosperous seaport that at-

[82] For instance: Dill, *Roman Society from Nero to Marcus Aurelius;* Salonius 20: J. W. Duff, *Roman Satire,* Cambridge 1937, 101–5; J. W. Duff, *Freedmen in the Early Empire,* repr. Cambridge 1958, 126: we may recall the traditional anti-intellectualism of the Romans: C. Marius was completely ignorant of Greek culture: Sallust *Jug.* 85. No doubt Petronius used Trimalchio as a figure for his satire: Sullivan 150–7 gives a balanced estimate of the whole question.

[83] 75, 10 suggests this: so also do the references to *ipsimus* and *ipsima* (75, 11) *cf.* the voluntary entry into servitude of one of T's friends 57, 4.

[84] Notes: 81, 83 above: also Herodas *Mime,*V.

[85] We may note that an absurd version of this familiar paradox is attributed to Bion: Hoïstad: 178. B. was reputed to be the author of a book περὶ δουλείας from which apophthegms on the subject may be derived: Mullach fg. l.

[86] 76, 9–10 *postquam coepi plus habere quam tota patria mea habet, manum de tabula: sustuli me de negotiatione et coepi (per) libertos faenerare.*

tracted people from all parts of the empire, there was a notable increase in people of freedman stock who were in high places in the community, though (unlike Trimalchio) their families only became established as a local ruling class after three generations.[87] On the other hand we know that *principes* ruled through freedmen, [88] who held high offices on the principial staff.

Much has been made of the view that Petronius despised and disliked people of Trimalchio's type. There is little evidence to support this. Petronius does not seem to have marked or consistent sympathy with any of his characters[89] – even the Encolpius who is possibly identified with himself. He shows comprehension of many aspects of human behaviour, and it is fairer to say that he understood Trimalchio rather than that he despised him. The portrait is a satirical one, and thus it has in it an element of attack, but there is little to suggest active dislike. On the other hand, Trimalchio, like the society which produced him, and like the literature which speciously (in Petronius' opinion) malnourished that society, is a fair target for mockery. There is a certain directness in Trimalchio's personality that Petronius surely did not despise. Trimalchio was ignorant but not decadent, intolerable company but not without humanity, indecent but generous, and by the standards of his time, not cruel. Trimalchio had his own form of *simplicitas*,[90] and though we have no reason to believe that Petronius would necessarily have approved entirely of anybody's *simplicitas*, (including his own),[91] he was surely, on the evidence of his literary skill as presented by the *Satyricon*, capable of making a connection between the ripe outspokenness of Trimalchio, and his own sophisticated outspokenness. Trimalchio is the reverse of Petronius' own coin – according to

---

[87] Meiggs, 70.

[88] Duff, *Freedmen* etc. ch. VIII.

[89] Sullivan, 265–7.

[90] The question of Petronius' *simplicitas* as suggested by the phrase of Tacitus *in speciem simplicitatis* which describes how people regarded P's more outrageous actions and sayings (Tac. *Annales* XVI, 18, 2) has been subject to many different interpretations: see Stubbe, "Die Verseinlagen in Petronius," *Philologus* suppl. 25 Hft. 2. 150-1; H. Bogner, *Hermes* 1941, 223–4; E. Bickel, *RhM* 1941, 269–72. Quite probably archaic "simplicity" is intended (Bickel) in some form or other. One of the best descriptions of *species simplicitatis* in modern literature is to be found in F. Scott Fitzgerald's *Tender is the Night*, Bodley Head edit. Vol. II, London 1959, 91: the outrageous, apparently innocent joke about the bathing-dress.

[91] Tacitus probably liked P's *apparent* simplicity as reflecting old Roman character (quite irrespective of what lay behind the appearance). For Tacitus' conservative tastes: Syme, *Tacitus*, 553.

Tacitus' description of Petronius' character. Trimalchio is a person of heroic dimensions, whose only enemy is the inevitable death which he has tried to buy off with the splendid funeral that his wealth could procure, and to which he looks forward with a thoughtless enthusiasm as if it were a day of personal triumph. Like a heroic character of epos, he is volatile and rude,[92] but his bark is worse than his bite. He threatens dire punishments to his slaves at various points in the *Satyricon*, but always allows the offenders to go free. His mercy earns him the appearance of magnanimity, and the occasions for its exercise may be supposed to have been contrived to that end, but nevertheless, his abstention from harsh punishment is real. Whether it is sincere or not makes little difference. The number of tricks and deceptions which he has arranged to startle the guests may suggest that the offences which he forgives are concocted. We have an example of the rigged offence in the case of the pig which the cook has apparently forgotten to gut, but which in fact is stuffed with sausages which look like entrails. The cook is on the verge of punishment, but is let off.[93] This is a very clear example of the theme of pretence that runs through the work. At all events, Trimalchio remembers the slave condition which he once endured. "Slaves are human beings," he says, and invites them to the table, where they succeed in crowding the guests off the couches.[94] It is characteristic of the usual attitude that the household slaves have the benefits of his forgiveness, but not the rustic ones. When the minutes of his estate administration are read out, we find that the country slaves are not so well treated as those who are in personal contact with their master in the house.(53) This agrees not only with the customary attitude of ancient slave-owners, but also with the rather limited scope of human sympathy that is observable in Trimalchio. Perhaps even more than other characters, his sympathy |is engaged by what is before his eyes, or happens to be an immediate object of apprehension. This is illustrated by Trimalchio's flirtation with his boyfriend, Croesus, in the presence of Fortunata. (64) He is insensitive to everything but the matter that is before his attention. This type of personality could concentrate intensely upon individual transactions of business from which his

---

[92] *Cf.* note 58 above: Petronius has this "rudeness" under perfect artistic control: Abbott points out (49–50) how the language and manner of Trimalchio undergo a change as he becomes more affected by drink in the course of the dinner.

[93] 49, 8–9.

[94] 71, 1: *diffusus hac contentione Trimalchio "amici" inquit "et servi homines sunt et aeque unum lactem biberunt, etiam si illos malus fatus oppresserit."*

prosperity grew. This is combined, as it easily can be, with the enduring love of property which has however, little in it of the narrow obsession of the miser. Trimalchio wishes to be like a prince, who can spend lavishly and not count the cost. He realises his desire for self-assertion by conspicuous expenditure from apparently inexhaustible wealth, rather than by the oppression of fellow creatures.[95] He admits slaves to the human family but he does not question the fact of slavery as an institution. His perceptions are short-term, immediately concentrated, and exclude peripheral distractions; his bursts of bad temper are connected with this trait; so also is his rudeness and his inability to appreciate the finality of death – though his attitude on this last point was common enough in all kinds of temperaments. For him, death means nothing but the glories of his funeral and monument, and he does not conceive of his ego being absent, or even attenuated at the occasion of his final public appearance. It is not final. There will always be Trimalchio. His rudeness is of a piece with the shortness of grain in his perceptive personality. The immediate is all-important, and the game of draughts must be finished before the guests are attended to. (33) So too, he says, the wine served is better tonight than it was when, a couple of nights back, he had much more important people to dinner. (34) Last century, and some part of this one, periods not distinguished for good manners, have shown remarkable sensitivity to Trimalchio's rudeness. A number of authors have criticised him for it. But his rudeness is simply shortness of grain and inability to comprehend more than one thing concentratedly at a time. There is also the rudeness of pure energy: we may be reminded of the rudeness of manner in the Elizabethan age, when people of high social standing freely behaved in the rough fashion of Mr. Walter Raleigh towards his father: "Box about t'will come to my father anon" – without any great harm being intended by it.[96] Certainly Trimalchio is not nearly so complex or vulnerable a personality as F. Scott Fitzgerald's Gatsby, with whom he has been compared.[97]

---

[95] Note 34 above; Schnur op. cit.: even if Trimalchio's fortune is in fact only of moderate size, he acts on the assumption that it is enormous, which is presumably part of the satire upon him and his kind.

[96] Especially the rough play at the dinner party in which Sir W. cuffed his son, who in turn hit his neighbour saying, "Box about t'will come to my father anon." John Aubrey, Life of Sir Walter Raleigh: Aubrey's Brief Lives edit. O. Lawson Dick, London 1949, 319.

[97] Paul Mackendrick, "The Great Gatsby and Trimalchio," Classical Journal 45, 7, 1950, 304–14.

Fortunata and Scintilla are the only female characters in Petronius who are not presented as menacing. They are pathetic and absurd (but not unsympathetic) ex-slaves or freedwomen whose husbands have become wealthy and powerful, and who are consequently a little insecure. Fortunata, Trimalchio's wife, is not necessarily (as has been supposed) of native Roman stock.[98] This suggestion, which was based upon her name, is not convincing, for her name ("Lucky") is precisely the kind of name that might be given to a slave girl. She has been a dancer, and is reproached by her husband in a quarrel, with this fact: "*fulcipedia*," he calls her – "hoofer".? Their quarrels are violent and bitter, but the marriage (in spite of Trimalchio's male concubines) seems to be a real one. In early years, we are told, Fortunata helped the common financial cause by selling off her jewels so that Trimalchio could use the money to make one more attempt to retrieve his imperiled fortunes – "at this point Fortunata did the decent thing,"[99] says her gracious spouse. In spite of her dubious past, or because of the perpetual insecurity[100] and social contempt which it represented, she has become the model of the careful housewife. Her personality is tenuous and without colour, and her tears and impotent rage do nothing but exasperate Trimalchio in their quarrels. He is also said to be sometimes rather in fear of her. (52, 11) Scintilla, Habinnas' wife, is more or less a duplicate of Fortunata. Her name is also of the kind of pet name, "Spark," that would be quite appropriate for a slave girl. She is dominated by her husband, but the relationship, as it is depicted in our text, does not give evidence of such extremes as that of Trimalchio and Fortunata. There is a certain comradeship between the two women in their situation of gilded adversity. They admire each other's jewels; they comfort each other against the drunken horseplay and infidelity of their husbands with their respective slaves.[101]

These respectable housewives are quite distinct from the other female characters in the book. The others are menacing and sexually dominating. They provide occasions for Encolpius to prove himself

[98] Salonius, 7.

[99] 76, 7: *hoc loco Fortunata rem piam fecit:* tribute is paid to her business acumen earlier in the text (37).

[100] Fortunata's low early status is attested not only by her husband's drunken abuse of her as *milva, fulcipedia* 75, 6, but also in 37, 3: *ignoscet mihi genius tuus, noluisses de manu illius panem accipere.*

[101] 67, 6–10: They examine each other's jewellery in a comradely fashion; 47, 12: Scintilla comforts Fortunata in her quarrel with Trimalchio. Both have trouble with husbands who have favourite boy slaves: 69, 1–2; 74, 8.

impotent; those who attempt to cure him with rituals, do so in a shame-
ful and terrifying fashion. These women represent the opposite pole
of femininity to the embourgeoised Fortunata and Scintilla. Quartilla,
the priestess of Priapus, treats Encolpius and his friends with similar
impropriety and sexual menace. She is contemptuous of their manhood,
informed as she is by the inspiration of a fertility deity whose power
transcends mere individual potency, and whose worship jestingly makes
light of it. The element of menace is also to be seen in Tryphaena, Circe,
and Chrysis. In a more intensified and absurd form the qualities of
Quartilla appear in Oenothea and Proselenos, whose ritual for curing
Encolpius of his impotence amounts to a painful, obscene assault,
almost more terrifying to him than Quartilla's minatory amorousness.[102]

The element of ritual and the influence of the malign god Priapus, to
some extent explain the aggressiveness of the women who are so closely associated with his worship. But other women such as Tryphaena,
Circe, Chrysis, and Philomela, are no less aggressive – not to
speak of the treachery and unreliability of feminine nature which is
implied by the folk-tale of the "Widow of Ephesus".[103] Encolpius, while
consistently falling foul of female anger, is none the less attracted to
women and wishes to be successful in his love affairs with them, but
he meets nothing but humiliation. Also, he is impotent in his homosexual relationships (140) except in the case of Giton.

Something about Encolpius puts him in a position of impotence and
contempt vis-à-vis the female characters – this something is whatever
has made him impotent. The aggressiveness of the women is stimulated by Encolpius – it is not an inevitable or usual characteristic of
womankind in the work's *Weltanschauung*. Others fare much better. We
might say that Lichas fared marginally better than Encolpius if we
had more information about him, but we gather that he has been badly
worsted in a transaction involving his wife called Hedyle.[104] His attitude to Tryphaena is far from being even positive, much less dominating. He is thwarted and frantic, but after the fashion of an ordinary
man and not one who is cursed with a notable disability like Encol-

---

[102] 134–138: description of a ritual which combines tedium, fear and pain
in a fashion that parallels the Quartilla episode (16–25), save that the later
episode is more fragmentary: the original text must have been a very minutely
detailed account of an obscene ceremony.

[103] 111–113.

[104] 113, 3–4 *non dubie redierat in animum Hedyle expilatumque libidinosa
migratione navigium. sed nec foederis verba permittebant meminisse, nec hilaritas,
quae occupaverat mentes. dabat iracundiae locum.*

pius. A more successful man in this sphere is Eumolpus. He presents a contrast to his fellow intellectuals. Encolpius is young, but Eumolpus is elderly; Encolpius does not create anything, but Eumolpus utters long tracts of rather boring verse, and even under threat of stoning, cannot be brought to desist.[105] Eumolpus is a wanderer, like the others; he is somewhat mad, but unlike them, his craziness seems to have some purpose, – even though the purpose itself lacks sanity, let alone honesty. He is buoyant, hopeful, full of schemes, where they are lassitudinous, and it is he who conceives the notion of passing himself off in Croton as a rich old man with no children who might well be a good quarry for legacy-hunters. He enjoys himself in a positive sense at the public's expense. He lives the life of an active and colourful rascal. His activity with Philomela's daughter, and with the boy whom he seduced while he was his tutor, testify to his potency.[106] He is not so much the victim of his own desires (as are Encolpius, Giton and Ascyltos) as the cunning manipulator of them to gain his own special ends. He resembles more than the others, a "popularizing" Epicurean type who regards the world as a place in which he must live, as comfortably as possible.[107] His only passion is for the recitation of his own bad poetry.

The power of Petronius' character portrayal, and the way in which it is wedded to the styles of speech which the characters respectively use, which is individual while it still remains Petronian, makes it the more regrettable that large tracts of the book are lost. There are, as it is, many minor characters who create their own atmospheres, such as the haughty steward who magnanimously forgives his fellow slave a whipping,[108] the greasy kitchen slave who impertinently challenges Trimalchio to a bet (they are supporters of rival racing teams).[109] The fact that they all speak the same language which is Petronius' own distinctive language, without any abatement in the individuality which they possess, may remind us of (say) Dickens, but would I think, remind Petronius' contemporaries of Homer. A writer of powerful communicative genius leaves his reader with a sense of the inevitability of his mode of presentation and context. His characters are all imbued with his peculiar thought and emit the special flavour of his own philosophy of life. This, I would suggest, is true of Petronius' portrayals of character.

[105] Sullivan 194–5: some of Eumolpus' discourse is possibly a parody of Seneca.
[106] 85–87; 140.
[107] See: Sullivan 110, 212–13.
[108] Notes 10, 93 above.
[109] Note 10 above.

SOME THEMES OF CONCEALMENT AND PRETENCE
IN PETRONIUS' *SATYRICON*

Notable elements of concealment, secrecy and pretence occur in the *Satyricon*. They are so prominent in what we possess of the text that they may well represent major themes in the original whole. If this is the case, it perhaps lends some colour, if nothing else, to the theory that in lost episodes of the book, Encolpius was expelled from Massilia as a φαρμακός.[1] Before we discuss the occurrences of these motives in Petronius' Satyricon, we must give some brief consideration to the background of Roman experience and custom that leads to them as they appear in this puzzling work.

The notion of secrecy was strong in Roman Life. The formulaic procedures and rigidities of Roman worship of the gods,[2] insistence upon literalness and uniformity in the verbal expression of laws, the power of *mos maiorum*, the strength of family ties, all imposed upon the individual a necessity for at least outward conformity.[3] These

---

[1] C. Cichorius, "Petronius and Massilia," *Römische Studien*, Berlin 1922, 138–9.

[2] Quintilian I, 6, 40: *Saliorum carmina vix sacerdotibus suis satis intellecta; sed illa mutari vetat religio et consecratis utendum est. Cf.* also the legal caution in such formulae as: *sive quo alio nomine fas est nominare:* Macrob. *Sat.* III 9, 10. *et al.* In the case of sacrifices, the precise purpose had to be named (*harum rerum ergo*) Cato, *Agr.* 139, 141. 7: G. Wissowa, *Religion und Kultus der Römer*, München 1912, 37–8, K. Latte, *Römische Religionsgeschichte*, München 1960, 47. For *religio* as a kind of *ius*, see the passages quoted by Wissowa 380–381; W. Warde Fowler regards the distinction of *ius humanum* from *ius divinum* (Gaius II, 2 etc.) as being a secondary development: *Religious Experience of the Roman People*, London 1911, 486–8.

[3] See D. Daube's careful analysis of some of the verbal and syntactic themes in Roman Laws: *Forms of Roman Legislation*, Oxford 1956. The exactitude of the expressions lent itself to parodic legislation such as the Lex Tappula: C. G. Bruns, *Fontes Iuris Romani Antiqui*, (ed. 7. Gradenwitz) Tübingen 1999, 117, Buecheler-Heraeus, *Petronii Saturae*, 1958 (repr.) Berlin, which contains also the *testamentum porcelli*. Unlike, for example, the Athenian political procedures parodied by assemblies of birds in Aristophanes' play, the joke in these Latin

characteristics are already clear enough when the Romans emerge into the early light of their history,[4] and it is almost impossible satisfactorily to separate cause from effect in an attempt to analyse why the Romans overtly admired certain types of moral personality. But it is also the case that public admiration of certain types could be accompanied by toleration of very indifferent private behaviour. The strict requirements of Roman society demanded more from the individual than could sometimes be given. Human weakness found egress in usual and unusual vices, but the pressure of society required that often these should be kept hidden, (sometimes by a conspicuous pretence of virtue), and that overt respectability should not be injured.[5] Hence the powerful moral tone, for example, of some Ciceronian speeches against the private vices of individuals in public life;[6] hence the moralising of Sallust who himself was far from being a model of virtuous conduct.[7] In fact the wholesale use of moral opprobrium in public life for the purpose of discrediting individuals tended to weaken the effectiveness of such opprobrium itself, and developed that atti-

---

parodies lies as much in the very precise imitation of legalistic forms as in the other comic circumstances.

[4] For instance the *lapis niger* (of about 500 B. C.) has been found to contain in fragmentary form what appear to be detailed instructions for the avoidance of *iuges auspicium;* cf. Cicero *De Divinatione* II, 77; R, Bloch *The Origins of Rome*, London, 1964, trans. Shenfield, 119. See A. S. Pease's note (ed. II, 77) on *iuges auspicium* in general, "M. Tulli Ciceronis De Divinatione Libri Duo," *University of Illinois Studies in Language and Literature*, Vol. VI, 1920, 160–500, Vol. VIII, 1923, 153–474, repr. 1963, Darmstadt.

[5] For awareness of the contrast between what respectability demanded and what actually was done, one might cite Cicero's defence of Caelius' youthful vices *pro Caelio* 39–43. Occasional visits to the *lupanar* were tolerated. Schol. ad Hor. Sat. 1, 2, 31 for the views of the elder Cato (R. G. Austin's note on *Pro Caelio* 48, Oxford 1952 ed. 2, 110; Catullus' marriage song, Poem 61 (references to the *concubinus* 120 etc.) indicates a similar permissiveness, which, it must be noted, was to be restrained after marriage.

[6] The attitudes of severe moral reprehension adopted by Cicero in his second *Philippic* indicate the style of moral criticism that was capable of being understood and was based upon some *topoi* (still recognisable at the time) about how people should behave. This is not to say that his ridicule of Antonius was in all its aspects entirely valid or justified: Syme, *Roman Revolution*, Oxford 1939, 146; *Sallust*, California, 1964, 84.

[7] If credence be given to the story of his adultery with Milo's wife: Aulus Gellius, XVII, 18, and to the identification of Sallust with Sallustius of Horace *Satires* 1, 2, 47–9, and the comments of Pseudo-Acro, *ad loc.* R. Syme's careful assessment of the evidence exonerates S. from everything but an unwisely pursued *penchant* for freedwomen: *Sallust*, 278–291. He points out also that nothing proves that Sallust was lavish in his way of life (283), though this is perhaps a different matter.

tude of indifference which was notable in late Republican times.[8] By the end of the Republic, such ridicule was part of the style of political oratory, quite divorced in many cases from the private attitudes of those who wielded it or endured it. Julius Caesar could jest in 61 B. C. that his wife was above suspicion,[9] but in an earlier generation, even the elder Cato had one or two murky habits which suggested that action could be separated from profession.[10]

Let us look at another aspect of the same matter: Roman *Weltanschauung* was in many respects magical: spells, incantations and prayers were binding upon the Roman's physical and social environment itself.[11] There were some important facts which were kept secret in case they should be misused to the detriment of all society. Such was the name of the tutelary deity of the city, whose name was not to be revealed at large on penalty of death.[12] In the First Century, in 82 B. C.

[8] To illustrate the professional indifference of the politicians: (i) Vatinius seems to have endured with good humour the attacks made upon him by Licinius Calvus (Catullus Poem 53) – in his career Vatinius was both fiercely attacked and defended by Cicero. (ii) Cicero (Plut. *Cic.* 29) had it in mind to marry Clodia (in 63 B. C.): he fell out with the Clodii on account of his part in the aftermath of the *Bona Dea* affair (62 B. C.) and attacked Clodia viciously in *Pro Caelio* (56 B. C.). He is still acquainted with her in 49 B. C. *Ad Att.* IX. 6. 3; 9, 2. and in 45 B. C., it may be this Clodia's gardens that he intends to buy (*Att.* XII, 38a, 2). For the discussion of this kind of attitude, Syme, *Roman Revolution, passim.*

[9] Suet. *Divus Iulius* 74: *interrogatusque, cur igitur repudiasset uxorem, quoniam, inquit meos tam suspicione quam crimine iudicio carere oportere;* also Plutarch, *Caesar* 10. These were the grounds put forward by Julius Caesar when he divorced his wife Pompeia after the *Bona Dea* scandal of 62 B. C. though for political reasons he did not press the charges against Clodius who had violated the ceremonies to meet her. Frohlich, *R. E.* IV, i, *s.v.* Clodius (48). Caesar's remark was regarded as a fine piece of wit, so inconsistent was it with his own easygoing conduct; M. Cary, *Cambridge Ancient History*, Vol. IX, ch. 12, "The First Triumvirate."

[10] The elder Cato, being a widower, had a love affair with a slave girl. This was upsetting to his son, recently married himself, with whom Cato was living: ἦν οὖν ἐν οἰκίᾳ μικρᾷ νύμφην ἐχούσῃ τοῦ πράγματος αἴσθησις, Plut. *Cato* 24.2. Cato sensed his son's disapproval and remedied the situation by marrying a young girl who was the daughter of his client Salonius (Plut. *op. cit.* 24, 3–5); Aulus Gellius XIII, 19; Gelzer *R. E.* Cato was at this time in his eighties. He had strong views about the adultery of women, and maintained a dual standard favouring masculine freedom; Aulus Gellius X, 23; Quintilian V, 11, 39. Our impression of his son's character suggests much more consistency and civilisation (if less energy) Plut. *op. cit.* 24, 3–8.

[11] Nature gods: Wissowa 23–28, 380; Latte 18, and Ch. V. *passim*. On the question of magic spells and superstition: W. Wagenvoort, *Roman Dynamism*, Oxford 1947, Ch. XIII.

[12] It was forbidden either to name this deity or to enquire whether it was god or goddess: Pliny *N. H.* 3, 65; Plutarch *Quast. Rom.* 58, 61; Servius ad. *Aen.* I. 277; Macrob. *Sat.* III, 9, 3: these and other references occur in Einar Löfstedt's

Valerius Soranus was killed, because, it is said, he revealed this name.[13] In the same century, the offence of P. Clodius Pulcher against the sanctity of the Bona Dea[14] in 62 B. C. caused a great disturbance, and however indifferent some of the principals in the affair may have been about the actual danger accruing from the violation of these rites, the fact that it could be made the storm centre of a significant political upheaval indicates that the "tabu" still had general influence. Other examples of tabu and euphemism occur: the obverse of secrecy was fear of secrecy. The Romans disliked the introduction into their city of foreign worships which involved secret rites and initiations.[15] Apart from powerful relics of superstitious dread, the Roman senate feared the potential of such groups for political and moral subversion.[16] The *s.c. de Bacchanalibus* 186 B. C. is well known;[17] so also is the problem presented by the introduction of Pythagoreanism into Rome.[18]

discussion of the question: "Tabu, Euphemism and Primitive Conceptions," *Late Latin*, Instituttet For Sammenlignende Kulturforskning, Serie A, XXV, Oslo 1959, 182. This secrecy was an effective means of preventing Rome from suffering as the result of an *evocatio* on the part of enemies: R. Bloch, 129-31; Macrobius, *op. cit.*

[13] A. Valerius Soranus was a friend of Varro, and was himself a noted antiquarian and scholar of language. His murder was probably political (Plut. *Pompeius* 10) though Pliny (*N. H.* III, 65) gives the story mentioned here, which might well have been a useful pretext for his killing. See R. Helm, *R. E.* VIII, AI, Valerius 345; Löfstedt 182 n. 1; Bloch 130; Valerius seems to have maintained a species of mystical monotheism which may possibly be exemplified in his poetry in the following fragment (Fg. 4): *Iuppiter omnipotens regum rerumque repertor, progenitor genetrixque deum, deus unus et omnes:* Latte 277-8, Wissowa 69.

[14] A goddess of healing: Wissowa 216 ff, Latte 228 ff, whose exclusively female rite was disturbed by P. Clodius Pulcher; we have no evidence that Cicero gave his evidence against Clodius in the resulting trial because of any deep religious conviction: the suggestion in Plutarch, *Cicero* (28-29), is that Cicero was constrained to give evidence by Terentia's influence, since she wished to prevent a match between Cicero and Clodia which would have entailed her own divorce. Cicero's attitude to the affair, as revealed in *Att.* I. 13, 3, 4 is not without humour though he is aware of the problems likely to be caused in society at large. See notes 8 and 9 above.

[15] Probably the Roman ruling group's principal objection to foreign cults and philosophical schools was that they were spontaneous in origin and not officially sponsored. See A. Toynbee, *Hannibal's Legacy*, Oxford 1965, Vol.II, 400 f. 412 f.

[16] Toynbee, 385, 391, 412, and Ch. XII *passim* of the same work. For the surviving text of *s. c. de philosophis et rhetoribus* (161 B. C.): Bruns 170.

[17] Bruns 164-166.

[18] "Pythagoreanism" which particularly emphasised the separation of soul from body was introduced into Rome in 181 B. C. in the aftermath of the Hannibalic wars and was quickly condemned as subversive, in spite of its legendary connection with Numa. Ennius declares himself to be of this school. It re-emerged

Distinguished figures such as the linguist and philosopher Nigidius Figulus[19] were involved in the movement. From time to time action was taken against *collegia, sodalicia,* and other groups that were likely to cause political trouble.[20] The Senatorial "Establishment"[21] (the term that Toynbee applies to it) apparently held that there was room for only one *"collegium"* in Rome, namely itself; but Roman affairs were controlled from 60 B. C. by what was in effect a really potent *"collegium",* the first Triumvirate, whose transactions were sometimes obscure even to the most experienced contemporaries.[22]

Clearly, the dichotomy between appearance and reality in both public and private spheres was not yet a stale or moribund τόπος in the late Republic,[23] and the Principate which succeeded it enshrined the

in the time of Cicero. Little is known of the form of this belief except that it was not Pythagoreanism of the philosophical kind; Warde Fowler 349–50, 380–82; Latte 268–70.

[19] *Schol. Bob.* on Cicero *in Vatinium* 14. Dio XLV 1, 4. Hieron. *Chron.* on 45 B. C. His religion or philosophy which he called "Pythagorean" had little to do with the genuine neo-Pythagorean philosophy, but was more likely a cento of Magian and native Roman ideas: Latte 289–91; A. S. Pease 12.

[20] The Tullian Law *de ambitu* of 63 B. C. against the illicit organisation of votes by these groups was not ratified by the senate: the Licinian Law of 55 B. C. *de sodaliciis* was accepted: R. E. III A, I, *s.v.: sodalicium,* Pfaff. See also Cicero, *Pro Planc.*; L. R. Taylor, "Voting Districts of the Roman Republic," *American Academy in Rome, Papers, Monographs,* XX, 1960, 122 ff. The widespread effects in litigation and politics of the ἑταιρεῖαι of Athens are expounded by G. M. Calhoun, *Athenian Clubs,* Austin, Texas, 1913, repr. "L'Erma" 1964, 40–96, 97–147; Lipsius, *Das Attische Recht und Rechtsverhalten,* Darmstadt 1966 (repr.) 909.

[21] This term first became current in the mid-fifties of the Twentieth Century to denote the academic-political-administrative continuum in British society: the members of this continuum were thought to be of similar educational background and to "know" each other intuitively or by acquaintance, and they were the effective rulers of the country. (See Fowler, *Modern English Usage,* Ed. 2. 1959, *sub. voc*). A. Toynbee adapted the term to his own use to describe the cohesion and continuity of office-holding families in the Roman Republic: *Hannibal's Legacy,* Oxford 1965; *cf.* H. Fairlie, *The Establishment,* London 1959.

[22] Cicero had been invited (by strong implication) to join the Triumvirs' party by Balbus in 60 B. C. (*Att.* II. 3, 3), but had declined to impose limitations upon what appeared to be his freedom of action. It is not absolutely certain that he knew what acceptance involved, though his desire not to be too closely linked with Caesar is clear enough. In *Att.* 4, 5, 5, (56 B. C.) he admits that he has been an *asinus germanus* in not realising the consequences flowing from the conference of Luca: M. Cary, *CQ.* XVII, No. 2. 1932, 103–107. In *Phil.* II, 32, he refers to the fact that the conspirators against Caesar kept him in the dark about their proceedings (*celatum me*): Plut. *Cic.* 42; *Brut.* 12.

[23] Pompey, Cicero's hope for preserving the Republican decencies, was also *adulescentulus carnifex*: Val. Max. 6, 2, 8; Caesar said he was prepared to reward and cherish brigands if they should be helpful to him: Suet. *Div. Iul.* 72, and his

paradox of claiming to be the Republic, and in fact being an almost autocratic regime. Comparably, prominent men of the Republic had been found to have secret vices: Augustus preached public morality and practised private promiscuity.[24] Julia was a great princess but at the same time a nymphomaniac: her daughter was no better. The acts which led to Ovid's exile were kept secret so successfully that it has been impossible for succeeding generations to unravel satisfactorily what the content of his *error* was.[25] The pressures upon the individual to dissimulate his thoughts, and to present a conformist front became more and more intense under the Principate, though conformity did not always safeguard its practitioners from the fury of *principes* and the greed of *delatores*. Therefore the old Greek characterological theme[26] of the man who seems to be "x" and is really "y" persists in Tacitus and Petronius. It has been suggested that Tacitus' delight in paradoxical characters was perverse:[27] even if this be accepted, we can hardly blame Tacitus for devoting some attention to one

practice bore out the sincerity of his profession. Examples abound in our records: Cicero has been willing to defend various scoundrels, e.g. Gabinius, Balbus, Vatinius, Syme *R.R.* 81, 144 and esp. 150; possibly Catiline (*Att.* 1. 2. 1) whom Cicero at one time had thought to be quite an attractive personality: *Pro Caelio* 12, 13. Here Cicero uses the word *admirabilia* to describe the conflicting good and bad qualities in Catiline, the same word used (R. G. Austin *ad loc*) to describe Stoic paradoxes: *cf. de Fin* IV, 74. In *Acad.Prior* II, 136, *mirabilia*, in a passage where bad motives are discussed as the causes of good actions: J. S. Reid, *M. T. Ciceronis Academica*, London 1885, 337; Cic. *Paradoxa Stoicorum*, Sall. *Cat.* 5. Some striking correspondences have been pointed out by P. Perrochat (*Les modèles Grecs de Sallust* Paris 1949) between Sallust's writings and the Thucydidean account of the devaluation of ethical value-terms in *stasis*, e.g. *Cat.* 52, 11; *Thuc.* III 82, 4. *Iug.* 41, 5: *Thuc.* III, 82, 8. *Iug.* 42, 4: *Thuc.* III, 82, 8. Roman legal language also distinguished (as one might expect) the difficulty of finding out more than what *appeared* to be the case: Daube, Ch. 4. "Judgment, he appears to have offended!" – the use of *videtur* etc. Also Tacitus on Piso, *Ann.* 15, 48, 6. – on false or apparent virtues *Hist.* I, 52, 11; 71, 4; article *species* (*specie* + genitive) Gerber and Greef, *Lex. Tac.* 1532. See also notes 5, 7, 10 and 11 above.

[24] Dio 54, 19, 3; 55, 7, 5; Suet. *Divus Aug.* 68, 69, 71. Syme, *R.R.* 425–8.

[25] J. C. Thibault, *The Mystery of Ovid's Exile*, California 1964.

[26] As a specifically recognisable genre, characterology emerges first of all in Theophrastus' χαρακτῆρες, though Aristotle has a considerable interest in human typology in *Rhet.* II, ch. 12–17. (Schmid–Stählin, *Geschichte der Griechischen Literatur* II, 1. 64: Ariston of Ceos, Aratos and later Philodemus the Epicurean wrote in this genre. O. Raith in *Petronius ein Epicureer*, Diss. Erlangen 1963, 20–23, emphasises the probability of parallels between Petronius' work and the remains of Philodemus περὶ κακίων, which must be modified on the grounds that Raith refers to Theophrastus as often as to Philodemus (review J. H. Kaimowitz *A. J. P.* 87, no. 348, p 480).

[27] R. Syme, *Tacitus*, Oxford 1958, 548. *cf.* note 21 above.

of the principal means of survival employed by his contemporaries. He probably had to adopt it himself, and possibly for this honest Roman-minded man[28] the "Lamarckian" effort must have been so painful as to leave him bitter.

Nero's reign began auspiciously enough.[29] Even when the first glow of beneficence had begun to fade, the *princeps* showed himself remarkably tolerant. In due time however, the expected crop of abusive poems[30] brought punishment upon the heads of those who were supposed to have written them. Also, Nero's artistic activities were protected from adverse criticism with the utmost care.[31] Frankness was impossible, even for the members of Nero's *coterie* of sympathetic intellectuals. Everybody, in Nero's view, dissimulated secret vices; nobody was honest.[32] Apparent frankness could never be genuine and must never be mistakable for such, as Tacitus' comment on the apparent *simplicitas* of Petronius testifies.[33] Unless the *Satyricon* was kept a strict secret from Nero, (which is unlikely on a variety of grounds),[34] it

[28] Syme, *Tac.* 553.

[29] For signs of such initial decency: Tac. *Ann.* XIII. 10, 2, 11, 2. Suet. *Nero* 9, 10, and the so-called *quinquiennium Neronis*.

[30] Lucan is supposed to have been the author of a *famosum carmen* against Nero (Suet. edit. Roth, 1882, 299–300). Vestinus, Tac. *Ann.* XV, 68, 4, and Antistius, *Ann.* XVI, 21, 2 also are said to have composed abuse against him.

[31] He was most jealous of Lucan and prevented the publication of his work: *Ann.* XV, 49. He was jealous of Britannicus' voice: Suet. *Nero* 33. He hired a most elaborate *claque*: Suet. 20: and would allow nobody to leave during his recitals, 23. For other instances, see Tac. *Ann.* XVI, 16; 21, 8; Suet. 21 22. He was supposed to have engineered the death of an actor called Paris of whose talents he was envious: Suet. 54.

[32] Suet. *Nero* 29.

[33] Tac. *Ann.* XVI, 18, 2; *ac dicta factaque eius quanto solutiora et quandam sui neglegentiam praeferentia, tanto gratius in speciem simplicitatis accipiebantur.* The word *simplicitas* probably intended to denote an archaic Roman virtue; for discussion of its meaning see H. Stubbe, "Die Verseinlagen in Petronius" *Philologus* suppl. 25, 150–151: H. Bogner, *Hermes* 1941, 223–4, E. Bickel, *Rh.M.* XC, 1941, 269–272. It is reasonable to suppose that P's *simplicitas* began to seem quite genuine and no mere *species*, once the suggestion had been made to Nero by Tigellinus that P. was probably a traitor: *Ann.* XVI, 18, 5.

[34] It is difficult to believe that the *Satyricon* could be kept secret from the *princeps*, since it would have been unsafe as a secret entrusted to any group of friends that excluded the *princeps*. What was secret would be liable to dangerous misrepresentation if revealed to Nero. If, as J. P. Sullivan suggests, *op. cit.* 91 the *Troiae Halosis* of Eumolpus (89) is directed at Seneca's style, there would be no need to worry about its effect upon Nero, who also composed a Τρωϊκά, (Dio LXII, 29), or to suppose that it would be regarded as a satire upon this poem, part of which was possibly recited during the great fire of 64 A. D. The theme was sufficiently common (Lucan wrote on it *Statius Silvae* 2, 7). It is surely consonant with the apparent rather than genuine character of Petronius' simplicity that he should

cannot have represented in a recognizable form Petronius' true feelings
about the emperor. Its allusions to Seneca and Lucan could be deci-
pherable with impunity and perhaps with applause. If in any sense it
were a *roman à clef*, Petronius must have buried the key very deep in
order to escape detection and to survive. On the other hand, its
representation of anomic life might have been amusing to a *princeps*
who was himself capable of tasting low life at first hand *incognito*.
We cannot deny the possibility that Encolpius and the rest were based
upon real persons encountered in the *"Mohock"* activities of the emperor,
and such disreputable hypocrites as Eumolpus, poet of the *Bellum
Civile*, must have seemed like a good hit at the "Stoic" opposition and
sententious Lucanism. Jokes against Seneca would hardly come amiss.[35]
But at the core of the work there could be no easily discernible suggestion that Nero was being ridiculed, and it was only just before his
death that Petronius committed his opinion of Nero to writing.[36]
What in fact emerged in the *Satyricon* was the fluidity, untruthfulness,
insecurity and ambivalence of Roman society.[37] I would suggest that
the picture of these aspects of society is not accidental: the *Satyricon*
is in many respects impersonal; it is not the work of a genuinely naïve
genius; its author was precisely aware of what he was doing, and of the
effects which he intended to achieve. Not only is this impression strongly provided by the *Satyricon* itself, but also it is clearly available from
the account of the author in Tacitus.[38]

Let us look at the evidences of secrecy and pretence in the *Satyricon*
as we have it. At the beginning of the *Satyricon*, Encolpius' speech
against the practices of contemporary rhetoric is praised by the
rhetorician Agamemnon for its rhetorical qualities.[39] The principal
characters engage in various shifts and tricks over the matter of the

sail close to the wind by essaying a satire on a theme treated by Nero, see note
31 above.
[35] Satirical references to Seneca and Lucan in the *Bellum Civile* poem
(*Satyricon* 119–124) would be likely to be well received by Nero: but see Sullivan
170 ff 182 ff.
[36] Tac. *Annales* XVI, 19, 5: *sed flagitia principis sub nominibus exoletorum
feminarumque et novitatem cuiusque stupri perscripsit atque obsignata misit Neroni.
fregitque anulum ne mox usui esset ad facienda pericula.*
[37] It is possible to imagine an analogy between the fluent movements of the
individuals of P's picaresque work and the movements of Epicurean atoms in
the void.
[38] Especially in his account of the artistic care which P. bestowed upon the
arrangements for his own death: Tac. *Annales* XVI, 19.
[39] 3, 1: *"adulescens; inquit "quoniam sermonem habes non publici saporis et,
quod rarissimim est, amas bonam mentem, non fraudabo te arte secreta."*

stolen coat with the gold inside it, but these and such incidents are
not significant from the point of view of our discussion, and represent
merely the small change, as it were, of the picaresque style.[40] The
first significant episode of the work which touches our themes is that
in which Quartilla suddenly (as our text has it) (16–25) bursts in
upon the group of Encolpius, Giton, and Ascyltos and informs them
that she has taken over the inn in which they are, for certain rites of
Priapus that she has in mind. When she claims that she wants to purge
her attacks of malaria, she has in mind quite a different disease, namely
nymphomania,[41] which she conceals under the pretence of malaria,
but this is only one indicator of the monumental bluff she imposes
upon her three captives. The accusation that she makes against them
that they have desecrated the rites of Priapus[42] may or may not be
founded upon an actual incident that was described in a lost part of
the book.[43] Whether it is or not, Quartilla's volatile personality, veering
from one pole to another, between hatred and favour, laughter and
tears, creates an atmosphere of mystification in which it is impossible
for her captives to be sure of anything, and which, taken together
with the assaults made upon their persons, and the aphrodisiacs which
Encolpius drinks (20, 7), weakens their hold upon the reality of the
situation in which they find themselves. The outburst of *mimicus
risus* (20, 7) is also calculated to confuse them, by suggesting that some
joke is being played upon them, not unlike the plot of a mime.[44]
They are not a party to the joke and they are not going to be informed
of its nature.[45] All this takes place under the aegis of Priapus, whose
sacra are supposed to be in transaction, and at the end of it all, the

[40] *Cf.* the incident of Giton hiding under the bed is compared to the Cyclops
episode of the Odyssey (94, 7). (*cf.* 101, 7)

[41] 21, 3. Sullivan 122 f.

[42] E. Klebs, "Zur Composition von Petronius Satiren," *Philologus* 41, 1889,
623–635: the idea that the *Satyricon* is a species of *Odyssey* with Priapus in the
part of Poseidon is widely accepted, with various modifications. Sullivan 92 ff.

[43] C. Cichorius, "Petronius und Massilia," *Römische Studien*, Berlin 1922;
For argument that the Quartilla episode as a whole belongs to Book XVI of the
Satyricon, Sullivan 45 ff.

[44] For the "mime" element in Petronius, Sullivan 219 ff.

[45] Not unlike brain washing techniques: W Sargant, *Battle for the Mind*,
London 1959 (Pan edition), especially chapter 9 on eliciting confessions. The use
of psychological tension and purposely induced anxiety to increase suggestibility
in a subject is well illustrated on page 139 by examples from George Orwell's
Nineteen Eighty-Four and the passage of Apuleius' *Metamorphoses* which shows
the hero's conversion to the worship of Isis; *cf.* A. D. Nock, *Conversion*, Oxford
1961, Ch. IX. It must be admitted that Petronius' characters are very easily
unhinged.

reader is left unsure as to how much of the material in this section (16–25) was really intended to appear as part of a ritual and how much was parody of ritual employed by Quartilla as a shield for personal orgiastic amusements. I do not get the impression that Quartilla's people themselves actually are supposed to know, and it is possible that the author simply wished to create an atmosphere of ambiguity. It is reasonable, I suggest, to hold such a view from reading of the text in its surviving condition: lost pieces of the text (were they to be found) could hardly reduce the impression completely.[46]

The *Cena Trimalchionis* is a masterpiece of social pretence and bluff, even if we discount the suggestion that Trimalchio's wealth is not so impressive as it is intended to seem.[47] Everything about Trimalchio seems to be designed to create an impression of his riches and social significance. When we first encounter him at the baths playing a ball game, (27) the arrangements both for the game and for his physical comfort while playing are exhibitionistic: eunuch slaves are at hand with a silver *pot de chambre* for their master's use during the game, (27, 3) so that not a minute might be lost; and a piper who played small pipes into his master's ear (as if telling him secrets) as he travelled home in his *lectica*. (28, 2–5) At Trimalchio's house almost everything differs from what it first appears to be. In the entrance hall there are only painted watchdogs (29, 1) which are quite sufficient to frighten Encolpius. The *dispensator* is barely persuaded from punishing an unfortunate slave. (30, 8–11) The slave has lost some clothes at the baths, and they belong to this person who deprecates their loss though he describes their luxuriousness in the same expression: his real concern is the carelessness of the slave. The punisher turns out to be the steward of the house, a slave himself, and the slave whom he nearly punishes is in fact the butler, who asserts that he will show his gratitude to the guests for saving him from punishment by providing them with especially good wine. (31, 2)

This little episode is too neat to be taken at face value. It has something of the mime about it, and an element of παρὰ προσδοκίαν. Probably it is so framed to suggest to the reader that he should regard it as

---

[46] The abbreviator of our material begins with comparatively full extracts and then about the middle of the *Cena* ceases to give running dialogue and records merely poetry or generalities: a procedure which suggests (among other things) that probably more than one book is represented in the material from 100 onwards: see Sullivan 35 ff.

[47] Sullivan 150, points out how small T's fortune is in comparison with those of the freedmen of Claudius.

a device of Trimalchio's to enhance his own importance. Trimalchio appears late at the meal, heralded by a fanfare, and preoccupied with a game of checkers (33, 2–3) he ignores his guests at first, and then compares them unfavourably with some that he had previously entertained. (34, 7) His demeanour is full of showmanship, even to the use of foul language over his game. (33, 3) All is intended to show him at an advantage to his guests. In small things, such as the eggs which seem at first to be addled to the point of near hatching (33, 5–8); in large assertions, such as his desire to buy Sicily in order to possess a coast all the way to Africa for his voyages (48, 3), he propagandises himself, moved, perhaps, by some sense of inferiority that comes from his obscure origins.[48] Because the eggs are not rotten, but full of well-spiced *ucelli*, (33, 5–8) we may be persuaded to take more seriously Trimalchio's larger pretensions, his official status; (30, 2; 71, 12) his reference to some apparently important Scaurus.[49] Many of his pretences are quite open jokes, for example: his silversmith Corinthus who makes true "Corinthian" ware (50, 2) and the act of freeing the little slave dressed as Liber (41, 8) and then claiming he has a *Liberum Patrem* at last. (50) The acrobat who falls on him, by an apparent accident (for how seriously are we to take the purple-bandaged bruise?) must be set free also, lest it be said that Trimalchio could be hurt by a slave. (54, 5) The affair of the pig which the cook has apparently forgotten to disembowel before cooking is of the same tenor. (49) The cook is about to be beaten, and in fact is already stripped for the purpose, when it is revealed that the pig has in fact been stuffed with eatables. (49, 9) This also could be regarded as a prearranged incident of the

---

[48] 29–30, 4; 75–6: T. Incited both by drink and indignation at Fortunata's jealousy of the affection which he has shown to the little slave, narrates the story of his career, how he came from the East to Italy when he was the height of a *candelabrus*, was the lover of both his master and his mistress, was left a legacy by his master, upon which he built his subsequent fortun. It is a fine touch that this should be triggered off by the incident of the slave boy, who recalled T's own youth to him: there is also the hint of history being perhaps about to repeat itself. On the question of T. and of freedmen and their wealth: J. W. Duff, *Freedmen in the Early Roman Empire*, Heffer (repr.) Cambridge 1958, 125-8. R. Meiggs, *Ostia* 70, 222–3.

[49] 77,5; Sullivan 150, following Friedländer (commentary *ad loc.*) points out that this Scaurus was probably a *garum* manufacturer known from inscriptions: the last of the aristocratic Scauri died in 34 A. D. However it is possible that Trimalchio was either (a) trying to bluff an ignorant audience with a high-sounding name or (b) deceived himself by pretensions to aristocratic connection on the part of his friend Scaurus. It is clear that P. wants his readers to note the name, and if this is the case, to be amused by the reference in some way.

feast. Another example is that of the two slaves with *amphorae* who come in engaged in what seems to be a drunken quarrel; Trimalchio tries to arbitrate, but each slave in anger breaks the other's *amphora*. Shell-fish fall out of the amphorae. (70, 4–7)

Trimalchio represents that ostentatious, conspicuous waste, that has been identified and analysed in sociological terms by Thorstein Veblen in our own century: he refuses to complain at the breakages caused by the dog of his favourite, Croesus.[50] (64, 10, 11) But this quarrel with his wife Fortunata has a genuine ring about it, and arises from the arrival of a slave boy whom Trimalchio kisses; (74, 8–9) all of which is perhaps too circumstantial for us to be able to suppose that the author wished us to understand that the disagreement had been arranged in advance. Little conceivable credit could come to him from a revelation of Fortunata's humble origin as an *ambubaia* (74. 13) except to point out how she rose in the world along with him. The appearance of an accountant to give a report of his properties and the business that has been carried on in them is clearly another episode which could be pre-arranged publicity on Trimalchio's part. (53) There is, after all, no reason why the accountant should appear at the dinner party, no matter how urgent his business purported to be. The contents of the report, which read like the *acta* of a town, give some foothold for this suspicion, especially as they are full of amusing scandal. Trimalchio's reactions are perhaps too smart to be intended as genuine, and they all seem boastfully to enhance his wealth and power.[51] And, to crown all, the whole household sings all the time as if in an opera. (31, 7)

The *Cena* contains interesting references to mimicry and impersonation of an everyday, rather music-hall kind, for example *tonstrinum* (64, 4), *lusciniae* (68, 3), *Muliones, circulatores* (68, 7), *tubicines* (69, 4) and other humble aspects of ordinary experience. Most striking, however, is Trimalchio's imitation of his own death. This mimicry is begun when he has his will read to the company. (71, 4) It continues in his excess of self-pity at the end of his quarrel with his wife. (77, 7) He dresses himself in his shroud and stretches himself out as if on his funeral bier. (78, 5) The guests are asked to say something agreeable about the departed, as is the custom at burials. Since one of the guests is an undertaker, and since he has his brass band with him, the appropriate funeral music is available: one hornplayer plays so loud that the *vigiles*

---

[50] A. E. Housman, "Jests of Plautus, Cicero and Trimalchio," *C.R.* 32, 1918, 162–4.
[51] 53, 1–10: there is nevertheless an inevitable element of absurdity in this matter which is related to Trimalchio.

arrive, mistaking the noise for a fire alarm. (78, 7) In the confusion, Encolpius and his friends escape.

An accepted view of Trimalchio and his friends seems to be that the size of a man's legacy and the impressiveness of his funeral ceremony and monument represent in some sense a summing up of his entity and a continuation of it after death. This sentiment emerges clearly in the remark that one of Trimalchio's freedman friends makes about himself, namely, that "dead, he will not have any reason to be ashamed of himself".[52] This point of view is not confined to Italy of the First Century A. D.; it has been known to prevail in times and places where religion provided very different expectations for Trimalchio and his like; by a strange perversion of eschatology, man survives in the public's recognition of the extent of his earthly possessions.[53] At this point I would refer to W. Arrowsmith's recent ingenious interpretation of the *Satyricon*[54] which connects the themes of luxury, food, defecation, and death, indicators of the decay and decline in Roman society. Arrowsmith demonstrates a distinct patterning[55] of these themes in the work, together with the sub-themes of sexual satiety and impotence, and he suggests that the author's intention is to indicate a cultural crisis, curable by *askesis* of the Epicurean kind.[56] Maybe: but in spite of their vulgar gluttony, these rough men do not suggest any awareness of

---

[52] 57, 6: *spero, sic moriar, ut mortuus non erubescam*: his legacy will be respectable. Trimalchio's pride in his prospective tomb is echoed in some of the epitaphs that have survived to us: R. Lattimore, *Themes in Greek and Latin Epitaphs*, Urbana Ill. 1962, 225–7. T's desire to exclude undesirable persons from his tomb, 71, 8, is paralleled by a testamentary exclusion quoted by Meiggs 223: *excepto Hilaro meo abominando ne in hoc monumentum aditum habeat*, though this is perhaps more comparable with his desire that Fortunata should not be allowed to kiss him when he is dead (74, 17).

[53] No trace of philosophy here, nor of the Hellenic dualism that affected the vague native-Roman notions of the after-world: material is all. *cf*. Arrowsmith's article cited at note 54 below.

[54] W. Arrowsmith, "Luxury and Death in the *Satyricon*," *Arion* Vol. V, no. 3. Autumn 1966, 304–331. *cf*. Meiggs 429, the anal preoccupations of the jokes in the tavern of the Seven Sages at Ostia.

[55] Arrowsmith, *esp*. 307, 309, 310: where very distinct patterning of themes is shown – not the less remarkable in view of the fragmentary nature of the novel.

[56] Arrowsmith 331: "As a description of cultural crisis, the *Satyricon* is as extraordinary an achievement as Joyce's *Ulysses*, and is as fundamentally bright, cheerful and gay." In support of this view, one can refer to Joyce's method of dealing with the cultural crisis that beset him, torn between religion, nationalism, and modernistic rationalism of industrial urban society: "exile, silence and cunning" – a not un-Epicurean attitude; also his "non serviam" to society at large.

crisis, but thoughtless vigour, social and economic expansion.[57]
Cultural crises tend to be the concern of intellectuals, such as Encolpius.
Their naïve denial of death's effects is not so much a flight from reason
as a commonplace of most cultures in the practice (if not theory) of their
living. The lie is really given to the intellectuals who are more really
death-directed than these philistines, and dwell more upon the destruction of their selfhood, and of the intellectual culture which has become
bankrupt and irrelevant around them. References to death in the
Cena, whether in stray remarks,[58] or the incident of the skeleton
passed around the table at the outset of the dinner,[59] are directed to
the apparently domesticated death of a traditional society, a death
that is not really believed in by the healthy, and is kept at the level
of a myth by many customs and devices.

Perhaps this acceptance of an "unreal" death struck Petronius as
unhealthy or unrealistic; but if he was so concerned about it that he
wished to celebrate the dangers and fallacies of popular thought on the
subject in this way, he would seem to be much more of an Epicurean
philosopher than otherwise would appear.[60] Or if this is not quite the
case, at least he emerges as a very sensitive artist with intense social
preoccupation. Fair enough, if we interpret thus his own avoidance
of everyday society and his nocturnal way of living, but if we recall
the manner of his own suicide, which in its deliberate details denied
the seriousness (and possibly the reality) of what he was doing, and
was an "Epicurean" mode of self-destruction[61] rather than a Stoic
ἐξαγωγή,[62] we may see in it a parallel with the pretended "death" of

---

[57] H. C. Schnur, "The Economic Background of the Satyricon," *Latomus*
18, 1959, 790 ff. Meiggs 70.

[58] *e.g.* 34, 7, 10; 42, 3, 4; 43, 8.

[59] 34, 9: Arrowsmith (308) probably reads a little too much into this simple
apotropaic charm: *cf.* the remarks about enjoying life while one can.

[60] In the spirit of Lucretius III, 935 f. or Epicurus *ad Menoec.* 126: ὁ δὲ
σοφὸς οὔτε παραιτεῖται τὸ ζῆν οὔτε φοβεῖται τὸ μὴ ζῆν. Arrowsmith's attempt to
interpret the "Widow of Ephesus" episode as enshrining a somewhat Lawrencian
love of life, in contrast to the death and decay themes of the rest of the work
goes too far: *op. cit.*, 328–330.

[61] Cicero *de Fin* I, 15, 44: the gentle withdrawal from life *tamquam e theatro;*
Lucretius III, 944; K. A. Geiger, *Der Selbstmord im Klassischen Altertum*, Diss
Augsburg 1888, 14; G. Highet, "Petronius the Moralist," *T.A.P.A.* 1941, 176–
194.

[62] R. Hirzel, *Der Selbstmord*, Archiv für Religionswissenschaft 1908, repr.
Darmstadt 1967, 77–78; E. V. Arnold, *Roman Stoicism*, London 1911, 309–312;
Highet 188; H. D. Rankin, "On Tacitus' Biography of Petronius", *Classica et
Mediaevalia*, Vol. XXVI, 1–2, 1965, 233–245, 241 n. 22.

Trimalchio in the *Cena*. Petronius conveys by the manner of his living and dying the impression of his own personal complexity, and if, in this work, he intends a moral, it need not be a simple one, nor one which has a single level of meaning.[63]

If the freedmen and merchants of the *Cena* share Trimalchio's traditional avoidance of the acceptance of death, the "intellectuals" are in a very different category. Encolpius, Giton and Ascyltos are given to morbidity at times and in the case of more sensitive types such as Encolpius and Giton, this leads to threats of suicide when they are faced with emotional situations which place too heavy a demand upon their resources. It is understood from Durkheim[64] and others that anomic people are given to suicidal instability, and it is a well-known characteristic of the intending suicide that he should turn inward against himself aggressive feelings that arise from his insecure situation, rather than converting them into energy that is directed outwards. In a "lovers' quarrel," (80–81) Encolpius finds that Giton has left him in the night and transferred his attentions to Ascyltos; he is so disturbed at this discovery of desertion, particularly after the intense pleasure he has just experienced with Giton (79, 9) that he thinks of killing them with his sword. (79, 11) Of course, he does not, and in the subsequent quarrel Ascyltos, the more robust of the two rascals, offers to divide Giton with his sword so that they should both share him. (79, 12; 80, 1) They prepare to fight. Giton becomes hysterical and urges them not to act like Eteocles and Polyneices on his account; (80, 3) with a dramatic gesture quite in keeping with the literary reference which he has just made, he offers his throat to be cut by both of them rather than be the cause of dissension. (80, 4) Rather than do this, they offer the boy his choice, and he chooses Ascyltos, thereby bringing Encolpius to the point of contemplating suicide. (80, 7) He does not commit suicide, but goes off reflecting neurotically upon his own misfortunes and defects, and when he seems

---

[63] Even apparently simple moral tales need not be simple: for example, Swift's satirical target in "A Modest Proposal" is apparently simple; the inhuman social and economic management of a society composed of human beings, but beyond this, the genre, style, tone and humour of the work conveys important secondary messages to the reader. Petronius' death was probably a satire of Seneca's, but it was possibly also a satire upon life's preoccupations as well as approaches to death. Arrowsmith has managed to find traces of an affirmation of life's importance in the *Satyricon* (*op.cit.*, 328–331).

[64] E. Durkheim does not distinguish "anomic" suicide completely from "egotistic" suicide: *Suicide* (trans. Spaulding, Simpson), Glencoe, Illinois 1951, 288; E. Stengel, *Suicide and Attempted Suicide*, London 1964.

to have decided to go back in order to kill the two people whom he now regards as enemies, he allows himself to be farcically deprived of his sword by a passing tramp. (82, 4)

The frustration and unhappiness are real enough and carry conviction, but the threats of violence against himself or others are not very plausible. The energy required to carry them out seems to dissipate itself in histrionics, and the murders and suicides within the group do not take place, but remain fantasies.[65] The element of theatricality in these incidents, indeed this apparent reference to drama (or epos) by Giton[66] may suggest to us that we are not to take them at face value, but rather to regard the literary and rhetorical "bookishness" of the cultural tradition in which the characters are immersed, as standing between them and the capacity for decisive action.[67] Their violence is directed inwards, and inevitably misses its mark in its secondary external manifestations. Encolpius again prepares to kill himself – this time by hanging – when Eumolpus runs away with Giton, (94, 8) but they return just in time to forestall him, and Giton attempts to kill himself with a blunt razor, and fails. (94, 14) Later when Ascyltos comes to seek out Giton, he ransacks Encolpius' room to find him, and Encolpius offers himself to Ascyltos to be killed, asserting that he knows that this

[65] Had Encolpius actually killed people? At 9, 9: *nocturne percussor* is an insult, and perhaps should not be taken as indicating conclusively that E. was a murderer: it is accompanied by references to his unsuccessful career as a gladiator which possibly may be intended as genuine; they seem to be circumstantial, – though not significantly: *gladiator obscene quem de ruina harena dimisit*. It may be that *hospitem occidi* 81, 3, *hominem occidi* 130, 2, is intended to represent the truth of E's past, but some small discount may have to be made for (a) the rhetorical style and (b) the fact that E. is speaking in the person of Polyaenus writing a letter to Circe.

[66] *Thebanum par*: (80, 3) Eteocles and Polyneices – probably a reference to tragedy and a mockery of a tragic idea: see Arrowsmith's note in his translation of the *Satyricon*, Ann Arbor 1959. The expression itself suggests gladiatorial combat especially in the word *par*: gloss on Petr. (*cf*. Stat. Theb. XI, 125) Burmann. *cf*. also Propertius II, 9, to which Gonsalius de Salas thinks Petronius may allude; *cf*. the riot on board ship, where *tragoedia* is mockingly used of Giton's pretense of suicide (108, 11; 101, 7); also *tragoedia* 140, 6. Another attempt of Giton to kill himself is rightly described as *mimica mors* 94, 15: its highly coloured dramatic circumstances and speeches (94, 9–14) come to nothing.

[67] Their author's "bookishness" was of a very different character, and was distinctly classical: he at least refers to authors such as Thucydides (?), Pindar (2), Plato (2), Sophocles (2), Aratus (40), Alcaeus (possibly) (34), Hipponax (possibly) (138). Latte, *Hermes* 64, 1929, 384 ff.; Masson, *Les fragments du poète Hipponax* Paris 1962, 150. Plato's *Symposium* was probably a model for the *Cena*: Sullivan, 59 i, who also emphasises that P. was in many ways a traditionalist, despite his boldly original handling of themes which were already "classical". See: Averil Cameron, "Petronius and Plato" *C.Q.* N.S. XIX, 367–370.

is the real reason for Ascyltos' arrival. (79, 9) This is a piece of bluff, since Giton is hiding in the mattress all the time, but the theatrical manner of the offer recalls the fantasy (if that is what it is) that is involved in the earlier attempts at self-destruction. The allusions to the Cyclop's Cave episode in the *Odyssey* give colour to the fantastic element. (97, 5–6) In the episode on the ship Encolpius begs Eumolpus to kill Giton and himself as an act of mercy when he realises that their enemies Tryphaena and Lichas are on board. (101, 2) In the razor battle on the ship, Giton threatens to castrate himself with his razor – knowing all the time that it was the same blunt razor with which he had earlier tried to cut his throat. (108, 10) Encolpius also threatens to cut his own throat, but openly admits (at last) that he has no genuine intention of doing so. (108, 11) Later (132) Encolpius threatens to castrate himself, when he is infuriated by his own impotence. However the Sotadic parody of Vergilian ideas which accompanies his attempts impugns the seriousness of his intentions.[68]

These attempts at self-mutilation and suicide have special reference to the characters of Encolpius and, to a lesser degree, of Giton. The literary and theatrical atmosphere in which these attempts are mooted is, as it were, an implication of parody, and points out that the characters have difficulty in taking even their own emotional extremities seriously as real problems to be squarely faced. A filter of literature and literary precedent keeps them both from actual self-damage, and from valid solutions of their problems. In another way, they might be said to be the victims of a literary culture which has long since lost touch with reality but which still maintained its prestige and its psychological dominance amongst the educated, though many people were now impatient with it. This is the culture denounced by Encolpius in Chapter 1 of the *Satyricon*. In the fantasies of its victims, and in their social dislocation and unhappiness, we are perhaps invited to see some of its results that Petronius disliked. The tragedy of people like Encolpius is perhaps that on no level are they capable of being taken seriously or of taking themselves seriously, though they are capable of suffering. Even their unhappiness appears to themselves to be some kind of *topos*.

Other concealments and pretences are rendered with broader strokes, with no less farcical, but more obvious, technique. The absurdities of the hypocritical old poet Eumolpus are of the slapstick kind whose

[68] See 132, 7: where E. addresses his phallus in poetry as a preliminary to castrating himself in despair at his impotence: see the deliberate absurdity on P's part of blending Vergilian overtones (132, 11) with Sotadic rhythms (132, 8).

proximate comparison must be mime, though the energy is more reminiscent of the Old Athenian Comedy.[69] His pretence of virtue is so much of a piece with the tradition of comic deceit that it hardly can be taken seriously as a significant concealment of the truth. The absurd and obscene consequences of his pretence in Croton to be a rich old man, with Encolpius and Giton as his slaves, (117, 4) are in the main stream of the comic tradition. His plan is to live off the *captatores* of which Croton is full, with promises of a legacy from his vast imaginary wealth. This is apparently successful for a while, but it has a dubious conclusion. (141) This policy brings in the sinister Philomela who, using the language of unimpeachable virtue, leaves her children to talk with Eumolpus, so that they may prostitute themselves to him. (140, 1) His final stipulation that his legatees must eat his dead body to qualify for their inheritances is simply one more joking pretence, tricked out in the language and erudition of the rhetorical schools.[70]

In the case of Encolpius and Giton, their attempts to disguise their identities on board the ship lead to nothing but comic misfortune. In Croton, however, Encolpius is apparently representing himself as a certain "Polyaenus" in his dealings with Circe and Chrysis. We may wonder what other aliases he adopted in the lost passages of the work. As Polyaenus, he is still affected by impotence, since the influence of divine anger or magic is not averted by a mere change of name.[71] We may presume that he changed his name for some other reason than to

---

[69] It is possible that 119, 11–13, in which the slave Corax's flatulence plays an important part indicates the author's familiarity with the Old Comedy (e.g. Ar. *Ran.* 8ff. etc.). Sullivan introduces and comments upon this hypothesis: *op. cit.*, 66–67.

[70] O. Raith, *Petronius ein Epikureer*, Diss. Erlangen 1963, 52, refers to Eumolpus' stipulation as „eine Kynische Posse": it is, however, something more than this, as the supporting arguments in 141 call in examples of cannibalism in besieged cities, and are developed in a fashion which is reminiscent of the "school" rhetorical themes that are ridiculed in Ch I by Encolpius. Cynics and Stoics were reputed advocates of ἀνθρωποβορία (especially in their πολιτείαι): ἐπειδὴ οὖν πολλὰ ἀνέγνως τί σοι ἔδοξεν τὰ Ζήνωνος ἢ τὰ Διογένους καὶ Κλεάνθους, ὅποσα περιέχουσιν αἱ βίβλοι αὐτῶν διδάσκουσαι ἀνθρωποβορίας, πατέρας μὲν ὑπὸ ἰδίων τέκνων ἔψεσθαι καὶ βιβρώσκεσθαι καὶ εἴ τις οὐ βουλόιτο... αὐτὸν κατεσθίεσθαι τὸν μὴ φάγοντα; Theophil. ad Autolyc. III, 5; Von Arnim, *Stoicorum Veterum Fragmenta*, Vol. III 750, p. 186. *cf.* 747, 748; 749 mentions its advocacy by other philosophers such as Empedocles and Pythagoras. This quoted passage resembles 141, in that it contains a social imperative and a penalty: the anthropophage (like the legatee) must be proved to have eaten, or in one case suffer loss of legacy, in another, be eaten himself. *Cf.* Raith note 84.

[71] Most of the references to Encolpius' (alias Polyaenus") impotence occur after he has arrived in Croton: 128, 2; 129, 5–7; 133, 3; 140, 11.

escape from the slave status which he had embraced on entering Croton. His original status is rather doubtful, to judge from hints in the text.[72] In the passages which deal with Encolpius' (Polyaenus') attempts to cure his impotence, the ministrants of the ritual cure, Oenothea and Proselenus, have, like Quartilla, motives other than religious and curative ones, and they turn out, like her, to be interested in sexual objectives.[73] We cannot be precise in the case of these latter characters whether they are intended by the author to seem to be conscious of the ambiguity of their motives.

It is difficult to draw a general conclusion embracing the significance of these themes. In spite of the caution that is compelled upon the critic by the whole subject, something may be said in general terms of themes which emerge so strongly in the surviving tissue of Petronius' work. The first thing to be noted is the atmosphere of unreality that the themes help to create: by this I mean not the absence of naturalistic and realistic detail, which is undoubtedly present, but simply that the characters principally involved in our fragments have very little sense of the realities of their lives or of society, and live in a world of fantasy. This "subjective" failure of the characters to connect effectively with the facts of their environment is the basis of an "objective" sense of unreality which the author wishes evidently to convey to the reader by showing him such an array of pretences, concealments, surprises. This atmosphere of apprehensive expectation differs from the absurdities of Old Comedy (for example), or indeed of mime and farce. It falls within some of the prescriptions of Epicurean literary theory,[74] but in some ways also it is reminiscent of Cynic *polities* which may possibly be referred to in *Satyricon* 141.[75] In such works, the contradiction of generally accepted mores is designed to refute if not to demolish the structure of existing society, and to reduce life to a state

---

[72] 117, 4; 126, 1–2: suggest that as Polyaenus he is still known as a slave. Tryphaena's remark: *meruisse quidem contumeliam aliquam fugutivos, quibus in odium bona sua venissent*, implies that Encolpius and Giton were runaway slaves, though this does not necessarily tell us that they were of slave status at the beginning of the original work. At 58, 1; 73, 2: it is clear that Giton is pretending to be the slave of Encolpius and Ascyltos.

[73] 138, 3: *solutae mero ac libidine*, seems to be clear enough.

[74] In its delight in the fantastic as distinct from the philosophically probable in its themes: Philodemus: περὶ ποιημάτων IV *Philodemus über die Gedichte*. C: Jensen, Berlin 1923, 15.

[75] See note 68 above where the views quoted come from Cynic *polities*: possibly the reference in Petronius 141 has been mediated by some such Epicurean writer as Philodemus (*Kolotes und Menedemos* 62-3). See also Raith, 52.

of philosophically acceptable animality. Since the *Satyricon* is a work of art, and not a philosophy, it does not directly aim at Epicureanism or Cynicism or any other doctrinal position.[76] It is in its social intent more likely to be a work of tentatively implied criticism rather than a tract of opposition. However, it creates a world in which nothing can be relied on, and nobody can be trusted. It holds a mirror up to the madness and anguish which are the characteristics that its author saw in nature and in society.

The author retreated from the light of day and preferred to be about his business and pleasure at night: possibly night was itself a philosophical retreat (of Epicurean flavour?) from the fluent, untrustworthy world of day. Possibly it was merely neurasthenia, or perhaps some more deep-seated and particular neurosis that induced him to avoid daylight.[77] One is reminded somewhat of the behaviour of Proust.[78] On a more obvious level, at night Petronius was simply free from unpleasant social stimuli, and it is possible that he was therefore more released from the inhibitions that affected any writer who wished to write about the human condition at this period. The themes which we have been discussing, if they refer to the society of Petronius' time, indicate that he was working close to, but yet within the boundaries of permissible literary expression. On this argument, the pictures which he has left to us of the dislocation and anomie of the intelligentsia, the Saturnalian analysis which he made of the mechanisms of social pretence, the sheer image of humanity that he made, deserve to stand not far from those of Swift or Proust.

[76] Sullivan, 106–111, vii.

[77] Such as scopophilia, as Sullivan suggested, *American Imago* Vol. 18, 4, 1961, 352–369; *Petronius etc.* Ch. VII, section iii. He quotes K. Abraham to the effect that such neurotics have an intense desire for secrecy and mysteriousness.

[78] Whom Anatole France called "Petrone ingénu" in the preface to *Les Plaisirs et les Jours* (a parodic title of ΕΡΓΑ ΚΑΙ ΗΜΕΡΑΙ). Also like Petronius, Proust lived a nocturnal life, and was an expert parodist, and we may see a scopophilic tendency quite revealed in the episode of *À la Recherche du Temps Perdu* in which Françoise surprises Albertine and "Marcel."

PETRONIUS, PRIAPUS AND PRIAPEUM LXVIII

In 1889[1] Eilimar Klebs argued that the god Priapus should be understood to exercise upon Encolpius in the *Satyricon* a malign influence comparable to that which pursues and discomforts Odysseus in the Homeric *Odyssey*:[2] in short, that Priapus is the equivalent of Poseidon. The parallel is generally accepted, usually with the reservation that it should not be pushed too far and that point for point correspondences between the *Satyricon* and *Odyssey* should not be expected.[3] I propose to discuss here this question of Priapean influence with particular attention to the possible importance of poems like LXVIII of the

---

[1] Eilimar Klebs, "Zur Composition von Petronius Satirae," *Philologus* 47, 1889, 623–635.

[2] Klebs suggests that Priapus is equivalent to Poseidon; and he also (634) regards the wrath as conferring an "Aristotelian" unity upon the piece. K. Bürger also stressed the influence of the *Odyssey*: "Der Antike Roman von Petron," *Hermes* 27, 1892, 345 ff.

[3] J. P. Sullivan, *The Satyricon of Petronius, A Literary Study*, London, 1968, 93 ff warns us against suggesting parallels that are so close. (Ch. III, section V). He also notes that allusions to the *Odyssey* are quite frequent in the *Satyricon*, viz. 97. 5; 98. 5; 101. 7; 105. 10; 127. 5; 127. 6–7; 132. 13; etc. He is of the opinion that Joyce's *Ulysses* is much more "a close and affectionate" parody of the *Odyssey* than the *Satyricon*, agreeing on this point with W. B. Stanford, *The Ulysses Theme*, Oxford 1954, 214, 217. See also Stanford's article: "Ulyssean Qualities in Joyce's Leopold Bloom," *Comparative Literature* 5, 1953, 125–136. Like Petronius, Joyce is at no pains to be explicit in referring to his epic model: J. F. Killeen, "James Joyce's Roman Prototype," *Comparative Literature* 9, 1957, 193–203. The need to expound the relationship between *Ulysses* and the *Odyssey* has certainly been recognised by critics: S. Gilbert, *James Joyce's Ulysses*, London 1930; F. Budgen, *James Joyce and the Making of Ulysses*, London 1934; Richard M. Kain, *Fabulous Voyager* Chicago 1947; R. Ellmann, *James Joyce*, New York 1959, especially ch. xxii, and other works. Possibly from the fragments of Varro's *Sesculixes* there may be inferred a version of the *Odyssey* that might resemble Joyce's in its indirectness: Stanford *U.T.* 268.

Priapea[4] which possibly represents in a general fashion a literary precedent and source for some features of the *Satyricon*.

No doubt the idea of a god in angry pursuit of a wanderer who has sinned against him confers a desirable unity upon an episodic text, especially when its finely divided nature is enhanced by fragmentation and the loss of the greater part of the original work. The temptation to accept some such a vertebral theme as a divine wrath against a "hero" is very great, but since it was first propounded[5], Klebs theory has

[4] The view taken of the *Priapea* is that they belong to the time of the first Principate, and not, as Bucheit has argued (*Studien zum Corpus Priapeorum*, Zetemata Hft. 22, München 1962) to the time of Martial. The question of whether or not the authorship is single or multiple is not relevant to the argument presented here. Whether their close association in the tradition with the lesser Vergilian poems is significant for their authorship or whether they are "Diversorum" (as some XIV century editor suggested M.S. Laurent, 33. 31), the individual poem *Priapeum* LXVIII represents a class of material which, though satirical and epigrammatic in intent, breaks the bonds of the species to which it formally belongs (Bucheit 101) and presents us with a sophisticated and scurrilous attack upon the epic theme. The indecency is not simply that of φλύαξ or of mime: it includes, but also goes beyond such rudeness, and in its main points reminds us of the *Satyricon*, which also breaks through formal bonds with similarly brilliant effect. "*Suspicatur Magnus Scaliger esse hoc Ovidii epigramma; cuius coniectura fretus Scoppius plane hoc adfirmat;*" A. S. Gabbema. This view would be confirmed by R. F. Thomason: *The Priapea and Ovid, A Study of the language of the Poems*, Nashville 1931, which involves all the elegaic poems of the *Corpus*. See Radford: *T.A.P.A.* 1921, Vol. LII, who opts for one author who was a good imitator, 148. Even so, it is impossible to be quite certain, though characteristics of Ovid are clear enough in the poem. The lines after 19, *quid nisi Taenario* clearly cohere with the introduction 1–8, and most modern editors regard the poem as a unity: Baehrens, Vollmer, *P.L.M*; Schanz-Hosius, *Römische Literatur-Geschichte* Zweiter Teil, 274–5; Teuffel trans. Wagner, London 1873, section 48 p. 38. Helm, *R-E*.

[5] See in particular H. Herter's assessment *De Priapo*, Giessen 1932, "Excursus de Petronio," pp. 315–317, which accepts firmly the importance of Priapus in the material that we have, but opposes (317 note 1) the view of Maass (*RhM* LXXIV 1925) that the mock *Odyssey* contains opportunities for seduction which are provided for Encolpius by Priapus and of which he is unable to avail himself. Herter says: "Huc enim si Petronium spectavit, historia finita erat, cum 140. 12. Encolpius a Mercurio in integrum restitutus erat." However, I do not think that 140. 12. need be regarded as quite conclusive in either sense, since it might merely be a false dawn of renewed potency which was due to fail once more in some passage of the *Satyricon* subsequent to this, and now lost to us. For such false hopes of recovery see 131, 6, 7, (and possibly 138, 3, 4); it must be admitted that there is a certain positiveness about 140. 12, which is persuasive. It may be significant that Priapus sometimes had connections with Hermes (and with other Phallic gods) and was thought to be his son. Hyginus fab. 160; Herter *De Priapo* 309, and Wilamowitz, *Sappho und Simonides*, 35, note 1, emphasise the differences. G. Bagnani, *Arbiter of Elegance*, Toronto 1954, 12, is opposed to the "wrath of Priapus" theory on the grounds that there is not enough material left to us to justify it. Kroll emphasizes the triangle of homosexual relationship between

attracted some criticism. Most objections to it have been justified in detail, but it is impossible to eliminate entirely the general notion of Encolpius being pursued by the hostility of some supernatural being, and the parallel provided by the occurrence of such themes in the Greco-Roman novel gives it further support. The impression remains, then, that the *Satyricon* is some kind of mock *Odyssey*.

When we come to look in the text for references to this divine anger, we have nothing so obvious as the clear and explicitly stated theme of an angry deity which occurs in Xenophon of Ephesus, whose novel contains an angry Eros, or in Chariton, where the hostility of Aphrodite provides motive power for the plot.[6] What we observe in the text itself are indirect references e.g. when Encolpius is afflicted with impotence at crucial moments in his lovemaking: the impotence is the infliction (as Klebs and others argue) which Priapus has placed upon Encolpius for some kind of desecration of his rites. In the Quartilla episode (16–26) wherever we place it in the plot[7], we find a distinct expression that the god's secret rites have been defiled: we are told what god it is and it would not be unreasonable to suppose that Priapus is of some importance in the work as a whole even on the sole evidence of this

Encolpius, Ascyltos and Giton as an important aspect of the novel's main theme, which is erotic. We may note that in *Priapeum* LVIII the God threatens those who are unfaithful to him with sexual deprivation, not with impotence. The men of Athens who resisted Dionysus at his first arrival were said to have been afflicted with impotence: Schol. Aristophanes *Acharnians* 243 (Dübner).

[6] Kroll 120. 7. refers to Rohde, *Der Griechische Roman und seine Vorläufer*, 397, ed. 1, 424–5, 1960 ed.; Rohde discusses the background of such divine hostility, 156 ff (1960 ed.), stressing the importance of the typically Greek dislike of passionate (or ascetic in the case of Hippolytus) excess; see especially notes: 156; 2, 3, 4, 157.

[7] Fulgentius attributes 20 (and as Sullivan points out, *op. cit.* 35, by implication all of the Quartilla episode to Book XVI of the *Satyricon* (Fg. VII). K. Müller (following Jacobs) regards as an interpolation the sentence *illa scilicet – rustico steterat* (16. 3) which would (if it were an accepted part of the text) bind the Quartilla episode to the material 1–15 and make Fulgentius' attribution hard to maintain. Sullivan 45 ff is inclined to follow Fulgentius and Müller, though he does not ignore the references to "robbery" (17. 4) and a "law suit" (18. 5) which might refer to the trouble arising from the theft of the cloak (12–15). His sensible discussion of the question (*op. cit.*) does not claim to contain cast iron proof of the "Book XIV" hypothesis. R. G. M. Nisbet, reviewing Müller's text, *Journal of Roman Studies*, Vol. LII, 1962, regards the argument that *illa - steterat* was interpolated to bind up a loose narrative "less than decisive" (228). The element of literary improbability that seems to be associated with the retention of the disputed phrase is by no means too harsh for the Greek novel(or the mimes) ; on the improbabilities involved in the novel: K. Kerenyi, *Die Griechisch-Orientalische Romanliteratur in Religionsgeschichtlicher Beleuchtung*, Tübingen 1927, 2, 24, 25, also 31.

one reference. (21, 4–7) Quartilla's menacing sexuality seems to frighten Encolpius and there is some indication that he may have been impotent during the preliminary attacks made upon him and his companions by her female and male attendants. There are references in this passage of the *Satyricon* to fear and passive exhaustion on the part of Encolpius,[8] and it is impossible to say whether these are indications of his achieved excesses or of an impotence caused by the god. Encolpius shows some hesitation about succumbing to Quartilla's attempts to seduce him while they are both watching through a curtain the consummation of the ἱερὸς γάμος of the children Giton and Pannychis.[9] It is possible, however, that on this occasion[10] he overcomes his impotence. If the Quartilla episode is in fact in its correct position and has not been displaced and fixed into an artificial sequence, then the succeeding examples of Encolpius' impotence gain reinforcement from it, but cannot be held to stem from it (if *ex hypothesi* we regard the wrath of the god as a prime motive, and not one that simply occurs in the 15th book). Because Priapus is angry with Encolpius, Encolpius is likely to have the bad luck to fall foul of Priapus' rites and there may be a cumulative element in his bad luck. But before this passage, earlier in the text as we have it, Encolpius is shown to be quite nervous of being in a brothel, showing indeed, a remarkable fear of the place.[11] There may be some truth (speaking within the literary "universe" of the book) in Chrysis' view that Encolpius is impotent because of his emotional fixation upon Giton.[12] With Circe, Encolpius suffers from impotence, and also

[8] Ascyltos also is affected by such fear: 19. 3: their weariness is attested 21. 7, but at this particular point it is not absolutely necessary to infer that it is the result of sexual excesses: 22, 1. In these passages there is a strong flavour of the farcical idea of travellers trying to get a decent night's sleep at an inn and being deprived of it by a series of absurd happenings.

[9] 25, 4–5.

[10] Just possible, if 25, 6. *abiecti – noctem* indicates satiety, but an intervening passage is missing so that the story lacks continuity. 20, 2: *sollicitavit – frigida* probably indicates E's usual impotence, though it could be the result of sexual repletion: but *cf*. 23. On this question, something must surely be made of the exclamation of Quartilla "*itane est – Encolpius ebibit* (20. 7): unless the effects of the aphrodisiac had worn off already.

[11] To which he has been led by an old woman instead of to lodgings: *et subinde ut in locum secretiorem, venimus centonem anus urbana reiecit et "hic" inquit "debes habitare" cum ego negarem me adgnoscere domum, video quasdam inter titulos nudasque meretrices furtim spatiantes tarde, immo iam sero intellexi me in fornicem esse deductum. execratus itaque aniculae insidias operui caput et per medium lupanar fugere coepi in alteram partem:* 7, 2–4. He is reassured however when he meets Ascyltos there: 7, 4–5.

[12] 128. 2: – *si haec non sunt, numquid Gitona times?* E. pleads that he has

with the son of Philomela of Croton who prostitutes her children to Eumolpus in the hope of benefitting in his will. (140) These episodes have references in them to the malignity of a god or spirit or to witchcraft, which are supposed to be the causes of Encolpius' impotence.[13]

In view of doubts about the original sequence of the episodes it is possible to be too particular in attempting to discuss and define the "movement" of the god's wrath. We cannot disregard the possibility that some god other than Priapus caused Encolpius' difficulties. However, it is not only in this group of passages that we find references to Priapus. In ch. 104, he appears in a dream to Lichas, to tell him that Encolpius is on the ship in which they are sailing: an act unfriendly to Encolpius. At the same time, Neptune appears to Tryphaena, and informs her that Giton is on the ship. This is not enough to prove conclusively that Priapus has a special interest in annoying Encolpius, as distinct from his comrades, but when it is taken with the other passages, it is reasonably indicative of a malign and special regard.[14] In the episode where the crone Oenothea and her contemporary Proselenus practise magic rites (of an obscene and painful nature for their recipient) on Encolpius to restore his virility, Encolpius, in a state of unreason, kills a goose which turns out to be sacred to Priapus. The fact that the anger of the aged ministrants, and presumably of the god, is bought off with a small sum[15] does nothing to detract from the seriousness of the god's wrath as a theme of the book. We ought not to expect too much seriousness and consistency: application of the god's anger need not be any more consistent in the *Satyricon* than the behaviour of the god Dionysus in Aristophanes' *Frogs* or of other gods presented in absurd contexts.[16] It is sufficient that the god's in-

---

been rendered impotent by poison:*"regina noli - contactus sum."* At 128, 7, there is the suggestion that Encolpius is impotent with Giton also:*"itaque hoc nomine – lectulo iacuit."* Circe maintains that if E. (or Polyaenus as he calls himself in this part of the book) can abstain from Giton for a couple of days, he will recover his potency: 129. 8–9.

[13] 128. 2: *veneficio contactus*: in 129, 5–7: Circe expresses very grave fears for "Polyaenus'" (Encolpius') health in a letter: *negant enim medici – tubicines mittas;* 133. 3: *numen aversum;* 134: *quae striges – deos iratos;* 140, 11: *sed me numen – invenit;* 139, 4 probably may be read in this way, but the text is not conclusive in favour of this interpretation (see note 5 above).

[14] Especially in the light of the poem in which the reciter, presumably Encolpius, (see note 17 below), identifies himself with other heroes of antiquity who have been subject to the anger of the gods (139).

[15] 137, 6, 7.

[16] As in (Seneca's) *Apocolocyntosis Divi Claudii*, where, to quote one example, Hercules is represented as rather a simpleton (*minime vafro* 6) as indeed is

fluence be apparent from time to time and that it cause trouble, like the Demon King of a modern pantomine, and there is no reason why the deployment of divine power should not sometimes bring pathos along with mirth. We may add that the poem in ch. 139 has a reference to the wrath of Priapus pursuing the reciter of the poem, who is probably Encolpius.[17]

There is enough in all of this to establish Priapus as an important power in the *Satyricon* as we know it, and it would be unduly sceptical to suppose that these references are being over-read, if we accept Priapus as a Poseidon equivalent in comic form. We do not need, for this purpose, to add the dubious testimony of Sidonius Apollinaris XXIII, 144 ff:[18]

> *quid vos eloquii canam Latini*
> *Arpinas, Patavine, Mantuane,...*
> *et te Massiliensium per hortos*
> *sacri stipitis, Arbiter, colonum*
> *Hellespontiaco parem Priapo,*

though indeed this, if accepted, would seem to clinch the association with Priapus. However, it would not be proper, on the evidence available, to follow C. Cichorius in his ingenious biographical speculation about Petronius' possible Massiliote origin.[19] The identification of Petronius with Encolpius, and the idea that Petronius (Encolpius) was a scapegoat ($\varphi\alpha\rho\mu\alpha\varkappa\delta\varsigma$) because of some act of impiety, such as impersonating the god,[20] possibly in order to seduce some woman, remain within the bounds of possibility, and one may respect the ingenuity of proponents of the theory, while regretting the absence of evidence.

Thus the god only manifests himself once, and that in a dream,[21] in

Heracles in Euripides' *Alcestis*. The author of *Apocolocyntosis* represents the deliberations of the gods as proceeding under the standing orders of the Roman senate (Iuppiter addresses the others as *patres conscripti* etc., 6). The whole tract can be classed equally well as Homeric parody or political satire.

[17] This is very likely, considering its proximity to a context in which E. has been afflicted with impotence and the cure of impotence (138).

[18] Fragment IIII, K, Müller. Buecheler, *et al.*

[19] C. Cichorius, "Petronius und Massilia," *Römische Studien*, Berlin 1922, whose view (438–9) is based upon a very bold interpretation of Sidonius Apollinaris, 23, 157: *Hellespontiaco parem Priapo* taken with the reference to the custom of the *Massilienses* at Servius on *Aeneid* III, 57, a comment which actually mentions Petronius. K. F. C. Rose's identification of Petronius with T. Petronius Niger is persuasive; "The Author of the Satyricon," *Latomus* XX 1961, 821–5.

[20] Cichorius, 440.

[21] Or twice – 17. 5–6: *Utique–invenire*, Priapus is probably indicated as *praesens* in the technical sense: Kerenyi 98.

the fragments of the *Satyricon* which remain to us, although his presence and influence in the background can be gathered from the passages which I have mentioned. I should like to delineate this presence a little more closely, before we consider why he should be in the *Satyricon*. In anticipation, it could be said that the answer to this latter question is brief and easy: namely, that Priapus was a somewhat absurd deity as well as being powerful and sinister, and that his obscene comicality suited well the general spirit of the *Satyricon*. This is so, but there is more in the question than this, and Priapus may well be a literary catalyst in a more precise way than simply by representing a mock of the Poseidon of the *Odyssey*. The god is not described in any detail in the *Satyricon*, but he is well enough known to us. Our earliest information of him (in a form separate from other gods in their fertility guises) is at the end of the Fourth Century B.C. in Lampsacus.[22] He is thus of rather late development in the history of Greco-Roman deity, — as far as we know. He came to Rome eventually,[23] where he was identified sometimes with Mutunus Tutunus (or Mutinus Titinus) a native Italic god of fertility. Though Priapus (as distinct from Mutunus) was more of a cultural fad in Rome than a religious power, he was revered by the people of Lampsacus above all other deities,[24] and in the Greek world his role was by no means confined to fertility in a sexual and phallic sense. He was the patron of sailors and fishermen of harbours, and of all those who were undertaking a journey.[25] If this attribute were emphasised in some lost part of the *Satyricon*, it would add piquancy to the notion of Priapus' hostile supervision of Encolpius' travels. However, in our text, the dream of warning that

[22] Herter, *De Priapo*, especially 4, 11, 70. *R.E.* XXII: Priapos Jessen, ap. W. H. Roscher, *Lexicon der Griechischen und Römischen Mythologie* III, 2; G. Wissowa, *Religion und Kultus der Römer*, München 1912, 243; K. Latte draws attention to the unimportance of Priapus (as distinct from Mutinus Titinus) as a major religious force in Rome, *Römische Religionsgeschichte*, München 1960, 331; though it would hardly be fair to deny his popularity in some quarters, nor the impressive spread of his cult through the ancient world from the Third Century B. C.: Wilamowitz *Der Glaube der Hellenen* (edit. 3) Bk. II, 320 ff.

[23] The identification of P. with M. T. is first positively made by Augustine, *Civ. D.* IV, 11; (but in 90 B. C. Q. Titus issued coins which perhaps suggested the closeness of the two gods. Most references to P. are of the time of Augustus, though it is clear from monuments etc. that he was known in Italy earlier than this time. Herter *R.E.* 1940. *cf.* Vahlert, *R.E.: Mutunus Tutunus*. The Catullus fragment *hunc lucum tibi dedico* etc. (see note 27 below) indicates interest in him in Republican times among the *poetae novi*.

[24] Jessen, in Roscher, *Lexicon der Griechischen und Römischen Mythologie* III, 2, 2968–9.

[25] Jessen (Roscher) 2974–6. Herter; *De Priapo* VI, 201–239.

comes to the traveller Lichas is the only reference to this aspect of the god, and even his function as the protector of gardens is not much in evidence, if at all.[26] To the Romans in general, Priapus represents both sexuality and gardening, but in Petronius, perhaps by the chances of our text's tradition, it is his sexual aspect which is most prominent.

Priapus became popular amongst cultivated Romans in the late years of the Republic and in the early Principate. The *poetae novi* were amused by him,[27] and probably his fame in Alexandria helped his popularity in this quarter. It is perhaps a little surprising that he was favoured (even jokingly) by respectable supporters of Augustus, such as Maecenas. Any such paradox is revealed as superficial, if we recall that the Augustan new morality was largely based on the "do as I say" principle rather than upon the genuine establishment of good example.[28] Only occasional scandals reached the Roman masses, but the ruling class composed of Augustus' close associates and the nobility at large knew of his own "Priapism," as well as the instability of the Julii as a family, and nobody would surely be more aware of the contrast than sensitive Maecenas, whose own wife was seduced by the *princeps*.[29]

Priapus is physically represented in statues as a small ugly male with hypertrophied generative organs. Sometimes he has the lap of his tunic full of the fruit and vegetables which it is his function to protect from thieves and trespassers. In the Roman times which we are considering, he occurs in his anthropomorphically perfected form. He could also be symbolised simply by a crude stump of a tree with a protuding branch, no mere abstraction of fertility, since many such stumps resembled those which would put forth new shoots when they were planted. In this monograph, *De Priapo*, H. Herter provides illustrations of a wide selection of Priapi, ranging in the degree of their

[26] Not in the surviving part, to be precise, unless Fg. IIII *et te – Priapo* (Sid. Ap. 23) is to be read in a literal way.

[27] G. Luck, *Latin Love Elegy*, London 1959, 86, points out that Priapus was a fashionable god among the *poetae novi*: Valerius Cato had a statue of P. in his garden. So too did Maecenas, perpetuating, we may suppose, neoteric sophistication. Catullus mentions him in his fragmentary poem *hunc lucum tibi dedico consecroque, Priape*, (Ter. Maur. 2754 ff); and Furius Bibaculus refers to Valerius Cato's Priapus; *si quis forte mei domum Catonis* etc. (Suet. *de Gramm.* 11, 2. p. 15); pp. 63, 65. *of.* A. Traglia, *Poetae Novi*, P. L. R. VIII, 1962. The most striking correspondences with Catullus in vocabulary are *Priapeum* 52 and Cat. 16. 1, *Priapeum* 35 and Cat. 16. 1. Thomason, 95–6.

[28] For evidences of "priapism" in the *princeps* himself see Suetonius, *Divus Augustus*, 68. 69. 71: Syme, *Rom Rev.* 425–8.

[29] Dio, 54. 19, 3; 55. 7, 5.

anthropomorphism from rough stumps and branches to highly developed pieces of sculpture which are instinct with a grotesque self-
consciousness that may tell us a little about the attitudes of their
cultivated owners.[30]

There is a wryness about some of these statues that is difficult to
explain entirely in terms of a studied crudeness and rusticity on the
part of the well-to-do people who could afford to establish them in
their gardens. In many cases at least it was not simply a question of
purchasing a well made or quaint obscenity and leaving it in the garden.
The statues were obviously the focus of Rabelaisian attention, and the
collection of verses, the *Priapea*, which is associated with these statues
is usually attributed to the periods of the late Republic and Early
Empire.[31] From the point of view of our interest in the Priapus of the
Satyricon, this collection is quite suggestive. The verses purport to be
uttered by the god himself: they are pungent and usually well composed, and those that appear in the collection show Priapus in a light
which befits the guardian of gardens and a god of phallic power.

Priapus is full of menaces about what he will do to trespassers and thieves of vegetables, and he respects neither sex nor age. His personality
is abrasive and minatory, and he also shows signs of what we might
regard as sexual mania. He has no doubt that his physical endowments
excite the admiration of all beholders, just as they stimulate his own
pride. The smoothness and skill of composition in most of the *Priapea*
indicate that Priapus has indeed been taken up by the cultivated class
at Rome, but though his literacy is no doubt an improvement upon his
rustic origins, his attitude and manners are no better. When he makes
puns they are blatantly sexual, and when he indulges in word puzzles
and acrostics, the result is invariably an obscenity.[32] Though this
literary personality of Priapus may be the composite invention of the
several writers of his epigrams (and it is not fully established that
several writers were responsible), he is remarkably consistent in his

[30] For the more rough hewn representations of Priapus: Herter, *De Priapo*,
Plate I, opp. 96, also his discussion on 5. 178 *et alib.* See also Wilamowitz, *Sappho
und Simonides*, 35, note 1. (edit. 2) Weidmann, Berlin/Zürich/Dublin, 1966.
Herter *D. P.*, ch. iv, *De Monumentis* gives a descriptive list of the representations
and statues of P. Many examples of Priapus (and related deities) have been discovered at Herculaneum and Pompeii: for illustrations of a characteristic range
of statues and other representations, many of which are quite sophisticated
works of art, see *Herculaneum et Pompeii, Recueil Général des Peintures, Bronzes,
Mosaiques etc.*, H. Roux, M. L. Barré, Paris (Firmin Didot) 1872, Vol. VIII.

[31] See note 4 above.

[32] *Priapeum* LXVII: the solution of the puzzle is *"pedicare"* cf. *Priapeum*
VII; Bucheit 85–6.

attitudes. If he is at all concerned with religion, then it is indeed what
Margaret Murray in writing of another phallic cult, calls a "religion
of the lower culture":[33] the only power is sex, which can crudely be
transmuted into violence: he is himself a repository of that power.
His sex is aggressive, and the pleasures which it involves are sadistic
and punitive.[34] There is no reason to suppose that the Priapus of these
poems would be in the least interested in any sexual relationship that
involved sympathy or love, since these sentiments would diminish
the hostile and hurtful element which he dwells upon. He makes a
virtue of his own blunt speech, despises intellectuals, and regards the
high romance of Greek epic as being motivated by downright physical
sexuality.[35] No word escapes his wooden lips about his appreciation
of the joys and charm of living, growing nature. The vegetables are
merely property of which he is the custodian, and he does not care for
them as manifestations of ὑγρὴ φύσις. He is unaware of his fertility
functions as a deity. The women who visit his garden to conjoin with
his statue are not worshippers (in his view), but seek merely an improper
satisfaction.[36] His magical fertilising power seems to mean nothing to
him: like many contemporary Romans, he is a sceptic, and seems to
regard himself (as such Romans would regard him) merely as a piece
of material with some sensual contingents. The only object
that impresses him with respect is his own phallus.

An unpleasing personality, suspiciously like some Romans of late
Republican and Julio-Claudian times, emerges from the *Priapea*.
It is easy to recall Catiline, Verres, and earlier, the brutal senators
ridiculed by C. Titius[37] in the time of Lucilius. The personal habits of

---

[33] Margaret Murray, *The Witch Cult in Western Europe*, Oxford 1921, 19–28,
for the phallic and sexual aspects of the cult, 175–185.

[34] The most obvious threats of sexual assault on the part of Priapus are ex-
pressed in IV,V, X, XII (the threefold punishment for men, women, boys,
Bucheit 87) XIV, XVI, XXI, XXIV, XXVII, XXXII, XXXV, XXXVIII,
XLIII, XLV, LI, LII, LVIII, which threatens those who are unfaithful to
Priapus with sexual deprivation (not impotence), LXVIII, LXV, LXX, LXXI,
LXXIV, LXXV, LXXVI. For sadism in the *Satyricon:* Sullivan, 250 f *Cf.* note
4 above.

[35] *Priapeum* LXVIII, especially 9–10, 20, 25–30 (and *passim*).

[36] *Priapea* VIII, XVIV, XXVI (especially) in which Priapus complains of
being exhausted by the assaults of the women of the neighbourhood. Also XXXII,
LXVI *etc.* For the illustration of the religious ceremonies in question see Roux-
Barré VIII Planche 27, opp. 124. For the Mutunus Tutunus ritual in Rome, see
Latte, 96; Vahlert *R.E., op. cit.*

[37] For Titius' description of the excesses of jurymen: Macrobius, *Saturnalia*
III, 16, 14-16. See in connection with this, A. Toynbee's comments in *The Legacy*

Octavian come to mind, as they are described by Suetonius: the rumours about Tiberius, the realities of Caligula and Nero, and in addition many others who make brief and discreditable appearances in the pages of the historians. The ambivalence and irresponsibility of the Roman ruling class in general is revealed in these poems.[38] They are over-devoted to the brutal immediacy of uncontrolled temperaments, and they allow their animal urges to overcome even their calculation of what is expedient. At the same time, they are greedy, exclusive and cunning. They cannot, and never could, regard those outside their group as anything but objects for cynical exploitation. Narrowness and cynicism were all too Roman and too frequent in occurrence among the *nobiles*, as Cicero, for example, knew well.[39]

More intelligent and sensitive Romans, like Cicero and Catullus,[40] knew where this side of the national character would lead. Men like Petronius saw where it had led, and he, after his fashion, recorded it, as Tacitus did subsequently in his historian's fashion, at a time when his explicitness brought him no danger.[41] The *Priapea* were possibly intended to neutralise by means of laughter the negative and destructive elements and residual strands of the unease which seemed to prevail in the last years of the Republic, and which were far from being extinguished in the new dispensation of the Principate, as the general account of its history abundantly shows.[42] Into the mouth of Priapus are put reflections which illustrate the fundamental brutality of a society which was civilised enough to support self-consciousness and

of Hannibal, Oxford 1966, Vol. II, 49–8 (chapter XV "The Challenge to the Roman 'Establishment' from within)."

[38] "The Roman Hundred Years' Revolution (saeviebat 133–318 B. C.) was the consequence of the Roman 'Establishment's' unconstructive psychological reaction to the Hannibalic War and its sequel": Toynbee, *op. cit.* II, 487.

[39] Cicero expressed this well in 60 B. C., in *Ad Atticum* II. 1. 7: *nostri autem principes digito se caelum putent attingere si mulli barbati sunt in piscinis qui ad manum accedant, alia autem neglegant etc. Cf.* R. Syme, *The Roman Revolution,* Oxford 1939, ch. XII, 162–175 *passim,* also, 44–5.

[40] Both Catullus and Cicero could be regarded as "provincials" (Cicero as an Italian *novus homo,* less than Catullus; for the increasing importance of people from outside Rome: Syme *Tacitus* Oxford 1958, vol II, chapters XLII, XLIII.

[41] Tacitus, *Histories* 1, 1; Syme, *Tac.* 145, 517, 558.

[42] Syme, *Rom. Rev.* 491–2, 506. 511–13, on the decline of the old *nobiles.* W. Arrowsmith attributes much importance to the linked themes of luxury and death in Roman Society as it is depicted in the *Satyricon.* He argues that the extravagance of wealth, especially in relation to luxurious foods, indicates a preoccupation with decay and a tropism towards death:"Luxury and Death in the *Satyricon,*" *Arion,* Vol. V. no. 3, Autumn 1966, 304–331.

literary culture, at the price of certain perils and limitations upon freedom.[43]

This ambivalence in the cultivated Roman mind is well illustrated in *Priapeum* LXVIII, in which the god sneers at his owner, a gentleman who is walking in the garden reading from his Homer. Priapus utters an obscene, anti-intellectualising skit of the heroic themes, interpreting the Greek words in terms of gross sexuality and with a distinctly Roman ear. Scaliger thought that the author was Ovid. There is no precise knowledge of the authorship,[44] but the suggestion of Ovid as the author fits well with the mood of an age in which men who pursued a life of fashionable cultivation, and were apparently unobjectionable to the regime (i.e. in most instances the *princeps*), were discovered in due course to be its substantive enemies, as much because of what they were, as what they did. This is what happened to Ovid, and in a cruder way, to Petronius. Ovid's exile remains a mystery in respect of the *error* which occasioned it, but that the *Ars Amatoria*[45] should have been used as a pretext for it does not seem improbable, in spite of the number of years between its composition and his exile. People whose insight seemed too subtle, whose wit was capable of discerning the different levels of significance in the behaviour and precepts of the authorities, were liable to have their apparently inoffensive lives brought under suspicion – not so much as in the case of vociferous philosophers, but there were fewer of them than philosophers. *Priapeum* LXVIII exhibits the two sides of the whole situation: the crude menace of essentially anti-heroic power, and the remoteness of the gentlemanly student of ancient heroic deeds from even such action as will defend his own values and position. But then, the time for action is over and he has his doubts about these values and that position: he is amused therefore by the worm's eye impieties of his Priapus.

What, we may ask, would this Priapus have said of Aeneas? He certainly ridicules the Homeric heroes with brutal vigour. He claims that he is a simple old rustic who is compelled to listen to his master

---

[43] Syme, *loc. cit.;* Ch. Wirszubski, *Libertas as a Political Idea at Rome during the Late Republic and Early Principate*, Cambridge 1960, 91 ff 97, 98.

[44] See note 4 above: the work might possibly be a parody by an "Ovidkenner" of an Ovidian poem. Vollmer's view was that it was by Vergil. Seneca *Controv.* I, 2, 22, implies (it is thought) that the whole book is Ovid's work. Radford (*apud* Thomason 84, 87) points out metrical similarities which would associate the *Priapea* with the *Amores*.

[45] See John C. Thibault's recent summing up of the various facts and theories that concern this whole question: *The Mystery of Ovid's Exile*, California 1964.

reading and has learned Homeric glosses:[46] his interpretations of these are extremely obscene. He proceeds to more general interpretation of the poems, and in this he suggests that if a Trojan male organ had not been pleasing to a Greek female organ (i.e. if Paris and Helen had not fallen in love), Homer would have had nothing to write about. Similarly, if Agamemnon had not had a well-developed *mentula*, he would not, when he was forced to give up Chryseis, have offended Achilles by stealing Briseis from him. Priapus then introduces the absurd picture of Achilles sitting in loneliness, singing a doleful song to the accompaniment of the lyre, and in such a state of ithyphallic misery that he is more tense than the lyre itself (*cithara tensior ipse sua*, LXVIII 16). This image is reminiscent of mime or of the *grylloi* illustrations in wall paintings.[47] We are also approaching the kind of absurdity which is found in the *Satyricon* in the scenes of sexual misfortune and frustation. More of similar spirit is found in the next section of the poem, in which Priapus goes on to consider the *Odyssey*: the subject matter of the *Odyssey*, as he points out, is very different, but he considers that the motivation is the same: *si verum quaeras, hunc quoque (Odysseus) movit amor v. 20.* The magic *moly* plant (μῶλυ) which Odysseus used to avert the power of Circe to unman him, is really his phallus.[48] It was this phallus (or *mentula*) that made Circe

---

[46] The study of Homeric glosses is mocked in the Δαιτελεῖς of Aristophanes, Edmonds, Vol. I fg 222, and Homeric epitheta are applied to incongruous objects *viz.* χναυμάτια πτερόεντα κτλ (fg 224). Apart from the false scholarship of Trimalchio (50, 5) we have the juxtaposition of pictures of prizefights with scenes from Homer (29, 9). The Greek intellectuals' names, Agamemnon and Menelaus (3, 27, 48 *etc.*) are further reminders of the epic, see also Circe (127, 129 etc.). Petronius regards Vergil (himself the author of obscene poems: Pliny Ep. V. 3.2) as a classic, and so he is mocked in Encolpius' address to his *mentula* (132.8). Scaliger's explanation of the glosses in Priapeum LXVIII carries on the robust theme: σμερδ. dictum censeo παρὰ τὸ σμέρδειν. Quod idem est cum ἀμέρδειν et μέρδειν. Itaque plus erit σμερδαλέος quam φοβερός cum tamen cathedrae Grammaticorum fere omnes φοβερὸν tantum interpretentur. Non obscurum quid ipse velit, ut autem suis, bovis, muris, stercus, sucerda, bucerda, mucerda *etc. etc.*

[47] For such grotesques: Roux-Barré, *op. cit.*, Planche 7; Planche 25 (p. 25) a bird-Priapus worshipped by other birds, an unusual monochrome. See also Planches 40, 41, 42: grotesque bronzes *etc.*. Pliny *N.H.* 33.1, *in poculis libidines caelare iuvat.* Planche 58: the cynocephalous apes and bear representing *Aeneid* 11, 507: the escape from Troy. Varro's *Pseudaeneas* probably had links with comedy.

[48] *Priapeum LXVIII, 21-22: hic legitur radix, de qua flos aureus exit quam cum μῶλυ vocat, mentula μῶλυ fuit.* It is interesting to note that it is Mercury who is the donor of the μῶλυ in the *Odyssey* and Mercury also who apparently restores Encolpius' potency in *Satyricon* 140.

and Calypso want to detain him from his homeward journey. It was also an object of fascination to the apparently chaste and modest Nausicaa, though Odysseus concealed it with a branch of a tree (LXVIII, 16) when he appealed to her for help after the shipwreck which had destroyed his companions. All the time (according to "Priapus") his mind was concentrated upon the intimate physical details of Penelope, whose fidelity was of such an order that she kept the house full of lovers.[49] Her purpose is to find out which of her suitors is most potent, and she invites them to a contest: *nervum intendere*[50] which is a pun, having the meanings first, of drawing the string of a bow, and secondly of committing the act of sex.

The poem is neatly and sharply composed, and contains none of the stylistic opacities that occur in some of the other *Priapea*. It is a worthy example of the tradition of Homeric parody: not only in literature, for we are reminded of the puffy and absurd figures of Circe and Odysseus that occur on Greek and Italiote pottery[51] which relate to φλύαξ and mime.[52] In the field of literary parody there are many jocular imitations, direct and indirect, of the epic, particularly of its style, tradition and manner. In addition, a number of quite effective jokes have been made on the themes themselves.[53] First of all to be mentioned is the

[49] For the theme of the unfaithful Penelope, see Schmidt (*apud* Roscher) *sub. voce:* 1903–1909–1910. The story that she bore Pan to all the suitors (hence his name Πᾶν) is found in Duris of Samos (Müller *FHG*, 2, 479) *cf.*. Herodotus 2, 145. Usually she is regarded as the very type of marital fidelity, Schmidt 1907. See also Stanford 217. S. Gilbert alludes to these legends in his exposition of the character of Molly Bloom in Joyce's *Ulysses* (*James Joyce's Ulysses*, 386, 387).
[50] Bucheit 101, aptly quotes Ovid *Am*. 1. 8, 47–8.
　　Penelope iuvenum vires temptabat in arcu
　　qui latus argueret, corneus arcus erat.
cf. Priapeum 63. I. A. Gonsalius quotes Hippocrates to the effect that the veins and sinews ἀπὸ παντός τοῦ σώματος τείνουσιν ἐς τὸ αἰδοῖον, as an explanation of the sensus obscaenus of *nervus*.
[51] A Boeotian "Kabeiran" vase (British Museum 93, 3–3, 1) has a scene painted on it with burlesque figures of Odysseus and Circe. It is possible, but not necessary, that some kinds of mime is alluded to; a comparable skit on the *Odyssey* is illustrated by a φλύαξ vase. A. D. Trendall, *Phlyax Vases*, Inst. Cl. Stud. Bull. Suppl. No. 8, 1959. 39, No. 79 Louvre K 523.
[52] For a possible parody in mime of the Homeric *Nekuia*, A. Olivieri, *Frammenti della commedia greca e del mimo nella Sicilia e nella Magna Grecia*, Naples 1930, 148, fg. 14. Olivieri thinks it possible that this may have been in some sort a model for D. Laberius' Νεκυομαντεία. (*cf.* the comedy scene in part I of Olivieri's book, 31, Epicharmus, Fg. 50, based on *Odyssey* IV, 242–258). Kaibel *Com. Graec. Frag. I.* 1899, 195 Sopater Fg. 14; 108–9 Epicharmus Fg. 99.
[53] *Parodorum Epicorum Graecorum*, P. Brandt, 1888; *Sillographorum Graecorum Reliquiae*, C. Wachsmuth, 1885, 37. Schmid-Stählin *Griechische Literatur-*

Batrachomyomachia, the battle of the frogs and mice, which is probably of Fifth Century origin and is a skit on the *Iliad's* heroes.[54] The *Margites*, which probably is of the same date, has left relatively few fragments, but these (like the *Odyssey*) seem to be about the adventures of an individual person called Margites.[55] From the fragments we get the notion that the central figure of the epic was an innocent in all human skills, including sex, and that he was at the mercy of events somewhat like the "anti-hero" of the *Satyricon*, Encolpius. Very much was made, we might suppose, of the absurdity of Margites' innocence in a non-innocent world. There is thus a tradition of Homeric parody into which the *Satyricon* in some sense fits, though it does not belong to this genre (or any other) in an entirely neat and particular way.[56] It has been suggested that Petronius was acquainted with the poems of Hipponax at first hand:[57] Hipponax himself was a parodist of the epic style and tradition.[58]

This brings us to a confluence, as it were, of the themes that have to

geschichte, I, i, 227, 401, 642, 644. P. Maas' article, Parodos in *R.E*; R. Reitzenstein *Hellenistische Wundererzählungen*, edit. 2. Darmstadt 1963, 30–31.

[54] According to the *Souda*, Pigres, a Carian of Halicarnassus, was the author of the *Margites* and the *Batrachomyomachia*. In the introduction to the "Contest of Hesiod and Homer," the *Margites* is said to have been Homer's earliest work (313). It is not probable the Eustratius on Aristotle *Eth. Nic.* 1141 a 2 can be interpreted as arguing that Archilochus knew of the *Margites* and considered it genuinely Homeric.

[55] Aristotle, Poetic 144b37; the scholiast on Aeschines *In Ctesiphontem* 160 says: Μαργίτην φησὶν ἄνθρωπον γεγονέναι ὃς ἐτῶν πολλῶν γενόμενος οὐκ ᾔδη ὅστις αὐτὸν ἔτεκεν, πότερον ὁ πατὴρ ἢ ἡ μήτηρ, τῇ δὲ γαμετῇ οὐκ ἐχρῆτο. δεδιέναι γὰρ ἔλεγε μὴ διαβάλλοι αὐτὸν πρὸς τὴν μητέρα. The folk theme of sexual ignorance in a newly married person emerges also perhaps in *Priapeum* III 7–9: *quod virgo prima cupido dat nocte marito | dum timet alterius vulnus inepta loci*, the last phrase of which is referred to as *Ovidianum illud* in Seneca, *Controv* I, 2. 22. (Thomason 9). The fragment of Hipponax which parodies Homer is (like the *Margites*?) a ψόγος directed at an individual: Μοῦσα μοι Εὐρυμεδοντιάδεα, τὴν πολυχάριβδιν/ τὴν ἐγγαστριμάχαιραν, ὃς ἐσθίει οὐ κατὰ κόσμον κτλ (Diehl 77, Masson 128). On the question of parody in the *Satyricon*: E. Courtney, "Parody and Literary Allusion in Menippean Satire," *Philologus* 102 1/2, 1962, 86–100. Radermacher R. E. *sub. voc.*

[56] Kroll, *Studien zum Verständnis der Römischen Literatur*, Stuttgart 1924, IX *Die Kreuzung der Gattungen* 223–4; Stubbe 1–20; R. Hirzel, *Der Dialog* Lips. 1958, II 37–8.

[57] Petronius' sources were widespread: A. Rini, *Petronius in Italy*, N. Y. 1937, 159. K. Latte suggested a connection between the rite described by Hipponax (14 A Diehl, 92 Masson) and that of *Satyricon* 138. 1. which was designed to cure Encolpius' impotence: *Hermes* 64, 1929, 384 ff. O. Masson agrees on the whole with Latte, but refers to Haas' explanation of H's poem (*Die Sprache* 4, 1958) as a ritual infibulation: *Les Fragments du Poète Hipponax*, Paris 1962, 150.

[58] See note 55.

do with the significance of the Priapus figure in the *Satyricon*. Given that in the portion of the *Satyricon* which survives, Priapus is an important thematic influence: in *Priapeum* LXVIII we have what appears to be a precedent for the entwining of the Priapic influence in the parody of Homeric epos, and the character of the god, as it is disclosed in this poem and the *Priapea* in general, expresses a menace, a delight in the indignity of offenders and victims that fits in well with the indications of his attitude in Petronius' work. I have also tried to suggest that there was a social reason why Priapus was popular with the Roman intelligentsia, and what he might have represented to them, though these suggestions must of necessity remain tentative.

At least there can be little doubt of the vindictiveness of "Priapus" towards Encolpius in the *Satyricon*. Encolpius is poor, bullied and buffeted, and is deprived even of his potency. His principal pleasure is that of a *voyeur*.[59] He is a dislocated and anomic person, out of place in the society of which he is at the same time a characteristic product.[60] From a literary point of view we might represent more closely the part that Priapus plays in his life as the harsh and aggressive sensuality, the unblinking and hardly conscious brutality, of success towards failure. Encolpius is the intellectual who has taken flight, breaking all the rules of society in his efforts to escape, but at the same time, incapable of breaking as many, as effectively, as society itself. In this sense, we might see *Priapeum* 68 as a possible missing link first between the *Satyricon* and society of the self-indulgent and hypocritical powerful, and second between the *Satyricon* and some other literary genres in Rome. We cannot say whether Petronius knew this poem, but he can scarcely have been unacquainted with works resembling it.

---

[59] In *op. cit.* ch. VII, Sullivan expands the ingenious argument about the psychopathology of Encolpius (whom he equates to some extent with Petronius) that first appeared in *The American Imago* Vol. 18, 4, 1961, 352–369 under the title: "The *Satyricon* of Petronius, Some Psychoanalytical Considerations." Sullivan's theory, in brief, attributes to Encolpius (and Petronius) a tendency to scopophilia, and is based upon the incidents described in *Satyricon* 24, 26, 48, 92, 132, 140 *et alib.* If Sullivan's view is correct, we may note that tendencies to scopophilic pleasures were frequent in Roman society. Tiberius is supposed to have had rooms decorated with pictures from the text-book of Elephantis, who wrote on σχήματα συνουσίας. (Suet, *Tib.* 43). Pictures of this kind have survived: Roux-Barré, *op. cit.* Planches 15, 17, 18, 19. 20, 21 etc. cf. Pliny *N. H.* XXV, 9. 36., Athenaeus XII. 548., Ov. Trist. II, 523.

[60] Sullivan, 119, warns us against making too close a comparison with moderns such as Jack Kerouac, whose position, he suggests, is much more ideological than that of the characters of the *Satyricon*.

NOTES ON THE COMPARISON OF PETRONIUS
WITH THREE MODERNS

In comparing Petronius with Marcel Proust, James Joyce, Scott Fitzgerald, I do not wish to propound the rigid view that similar states of society produce similar artists, (though this has something to do with the question), or that any of the three Twentieth Century authors was dominated by a direct literary influence of the First Century A. D. though it is clear that all were to some degree affected by it. Joyce took Homer as his model, and so did Petronius.[1] Fitzgerald took Petronius as his model for *The Great Gatsby*,[2] and produced something as much Homeric as Petronian. Proust was, in his early days, called a "Pétrone ingénu" by Anatole France,[3] but we cannot discern how detailed the comparison was intended to be. Yet "Petronian" characteristics are observable in all three, both in their lives (taking Tacitus' account of Petronius[4] as our main biographical

[1] J. F. Killeen, "James Joyce's Roman Prototype", *Comparative Literature*, Vol. IX, 1957, No. 3, 193–203. E. Klebs, "Zur Composition von Petronius Satirae" *Philologus* 47, 1889. 623–35. *Cf.* for other source material of *Ulysses*: Attila Fäj, "Byzantine and Hungarian Models of 'Ulysses' and 'Finnegans Wake,'" *Arcadia, Zeitschrift für Vergleichende Literaturwissenschaft*, Bd. 3, 1. 1968, 48–72.

[2] Paul MacKendrick, "The Great Gatsby and Trimalchio," *Classical Journal* 45, 7, 1950, 307-314.

[3] In the preface to Marcel Proust's *Les Plaisirs et les Jours*.

[4] Tac. *Annales* XVI, 18, 1–195 *De C. Petronio pauca supra repetenda sunt. nam illi dies per somnum, nox officiis et oblectamentis vitae transigebatur; utque alios industria, ita hunc ignavia ad famam protulerat, habebaturque non ganeo et profligator, ut plerique sua haurientium, sed erudito luxu. ac dicta factaque eius quanto solutiora et quandam sui neglegentiam praeferentia, tanto gratius in speciem simplicitatis accipiebantur. proconsul tamen Bithynia et mox consul vigentem se ac parem negotiis ostendit. dein revolutus ad vitia seu vitiorum imitatione inter paucos familiarium Neroni adsumptus est elegantiae arbiter, dum nihil amoenum et molle adfluentia putat nisi quod ei Petronius adprobavisset. unde invidia Tigellini quasi adversus aemulum et scientia voluptatum potiorem. ergo crudelitatem principis cui ceterae libidines cedebant, adgreditur, amicitiam Scaevini Petronio obiectans, corrupto ad indicium servo ademptaque defensione et maiore parte familiae in vincla*

text about the ancient author) and in the character of their works.[5]

My principal suggestion in the discussion which follows is that comparison with modern literary work is to some extent packaged into the task of reading works of the classical past. This is also my principal justification for teasing out similarities between individuals of whose lives the outer and inner dynamics may be incommensurable in many respects. This may be so in many instances, but I would suggest that there are noteworthy outcrops of similarity in these authors. The literary (and personal) isotopism that the four have in common will, it is hoped, emerge. In psychological, or rather "characterological" terms, Petronius as man and writer has much in him that seems familiar to inhabitants of our own dislocated century.[6] We may note as a recurrent *topos* the instability of some of his characters, less gifted than some of the wilder "Vaganten" of the Middle Ages, but no worse educated, no less aware of a society which they have rejected than were the people of Kerouac,[7] or the Beats,[8] whose labile *psychai*

---

rapta. Forte illis diebus Campaniam petiverat Caesar, et Cumam usque progressus Petronius illic attinebatur; nec tulit ultra timoris aut spei moras. Neque tamen praeceps vitam expulit, sed incisas venas, ut libitum, obligatas aperire rursum et adloqui amicos, non per seria aut quibus gloriam constantiae peteret. audiebatque referentis nihil de immortalitate animae et sapientium placitis, sed levia carmina et faciles versus. servorum aliis largitione, quosdam verberibus adfecit. iniit epulas, somno indulsit, ut quamquam coacta mors fortuitae similis esset. ne codicillis quidem, quod plerique pereuntium, Neronem aut Tigellinum aut quem alium potentium adulatus est, sed flagitia principis sub nominibus exoletorum feminarumque et novitatem cuiusque stupri perscripsit atque obsignata misit Neroni. fregitque anulum, ne mox usui esset ad facienda pericula.

[5] Erich Auerbach, *Mimesis* esp. 27–30, but he draws attention (32) to the absence of a serious social or economic background to the characterisation.

[6] *Cf.* Holbrook Jackson's *The Eighteen Nineties*, London 1913: a portrait of a period, the "Nineties" of last century, which was deliberately conceived as a set piece of "decadence" by the historically and critically sophisticated intellectual group. It was an era that regarded Petronius as one of its literary ancestors (107, ed. 2. 1931)

[7] Sullivan, 119, is cautious about making comparisons between Petronius and, for example, such writers as Kerouac, on the grounds that the Roman writer is far less ideological, and this chimes with the point of view expressed by Erich Auerbach, *Mimesis* trans. Trask, Princeton 1953, 47, where he says of a comparison between Petronius and Proust, "but such comparisons with works of modern realism are never quite to the point, because the latter contain far more in the way of serious problems." Auerbach's view (32) is that ancient society did not have to be explained, but was accepted. The suggestion is, that when we come to compare a work like the *Satyricon* with a modern novel, be it of Proust or Kerouac, a whole dimension is missing. I cannot myself subscribe to this differentiation: what is missing is a knowledge of ancient society which is as comprehensive as our knowledge of our own; an author's awareness of his society, or his tendency

remind us not only of the *Satyricon*, but in some respects of Homer's heroes. Nor must we discount the possibility that such people may presage a departure from "visual" rationalising man of Western classical culture.[9] Joyce's latest work, for example, not only goes back to the pre-Homeric oral stage of *epos*; it also can be argued to retreat further into an age of circumambient magic of which language was a constituent rather than a medium.[10]

First of all, consider Petronius' *Nachleben* and influence: References to him in ancient authors are few: possibly his book was under some

to reflect aspects of it in sensitive records is a different matter; "the beats" are certainly less well equipped with ideology than were ancient Cynics, and their chosen art form is literature: see Frank A. Butler's rather hostile article "On the beat nature of Beat," *American Scholar* vol. 30, 1961, 79–92. Beats are "ideologically" non-ideological and anomic: Elwin H. Powell, note 8, below.

[8] Arnold M. Rose (ed.), *Human Behaviour and Social Process*; *an interactionist approach*, London 1962: Elwin H. Powell, ch. 19 *Beyond Utopia:* The Beat Generation as a challenge for the sociology of knowledge, stresses the absence of ideology in this movement (361) (as against Sullivan's view note 7 above), and paints a not un-Petronian picture of "reason held in abeyance" and "the pursuit of long-range goods is abandoned for the pleasures and the anguish of the moment."

[9] E. R. Dodds, *The Greeks and the Irrational*, California 1951 ch, I and II, on the loosely realised psychological textures of Homeric heroes. The personae of the *epos* are clearly neither literate, nor were they in their pre-Homeric form (if we may postulate this) originally the productions of a literate society. Reading silently in the modern sense was scarcely known in the ancient world, in which the spoken word predominated: though this is not to say that there was little literacy. On the importance of oral presentation of works of literature: F. G. Kenyon, *Books and Readers in the Ancient World*, Oxford 1932 12–16 – but books were widely used in Classical times: 22–24. See further, W. B. Stanford, *The Sounds of Greek*, California 1967, ch. I "The Primacy of the Spoken Word;" E. Norden, *Die Antike Kunstprosa I* Einleitung, (referred to by Stanford, 20, n 4, and many other works on the subject *ad loc.*). It may be recalled that the whole point of the Acontius/Cydippe story in Catullus 65 is that Cydippe should read the inscription on the apple aloud and not *tacite. Cf.* the quotation from Beckett in note 10 below.

[10] A monistic approach to literature of a predominantly or partly oral transmission is implied by Marshall McLuhan in his *Understanding Media*, 1964. Plato's doubts about the ontological status of literature and drama are also suggestive in this connection, also earlier "magical" views of poetry etc. R. C. Elliott, *The Power of Satire*, Princeton 1960, esp. 128; S. Beckett, on Joyce's "work in progress": "Examination" etc. London 1937 p. 14, "Here form is content, content is form. You complain that this stuff is not written in English. It is not written at all. It is not to be read, or rather it is not only to be read. It is to be looked at and listened to. His writing is not about something, it is that something itself." However, it has been agreed that Joyce's *Ulysses*, unlike Homer's *epos*, is not organised in memory and unfolded in time, but both organised and unfolded in what we may call technological space: on printed pages for which it was designed from the beginning: Hugh Kenner, *Flaubert, Joyce and Beckett, The Stoic Comedians*, London 1966, 35.

kind of ban, which sent it underground for some time after his death.[11] Almost certainly, his work was of such a kind that the ancient world found it difficult to place within the range of accepted art-forms.[12] Tacitus and Pliny, closest to him in time, ignore the *Satyricon*. This is not strange in the case of the former, and in the relevant passage the latter is not primarily concerned with literature.[13] Perhaps it is more than mere accident that other writers who mention him refer to special aspects of his work and show no general grasp of its spirit. Attempts have been made to show his influence upon Martial, or Martial's influence upon him.[14] He is mentioned (probably) by Sidonius Apollinaris.[15] Macrobius[16] refers to him as a writer of amatory *casus*, like

[11] Probably it seemed worthy of suppression only after its author fell into disfavour. Books of disapproved authors could be burned: Tac. *Agr.* 2; Pliny *Ep.* VII, 19, 5, on the preservation of an exemplar of Helvidius' book by his wife; Tac. *Annales* IV 346. Cremutius Cordus' work was burned: F. A. Marx, "Tacitus und die Literatur der exitus illustrium virorum," *Philologus* Bd. XLVI, 1937, 83–103, 87 f; Holbrook Jackson, *The Fear of Books*, London 1932, chs. I and II. See also: G. W. Clarke *op. cit.* esp. references in notes 7, 8, 9. Clarke argues that the practice had its remote origin in sympathetic magic.

[12] See George Gellie, "A Comment on Petronius," *A.U.M.L.A.* 10, 1959, 89–100, 98; B. E. Perry, *The Ancient Romances: A Literary-Historical Account of their Origins*, California 1967, 187, stresses that there is no need of a precedent for Petronius' work when one can point to the *Margites*.

[13] Tacitus does not allude to Seneca's tragedies as such, presumably because they are irrelevant in his view to his political analysis of Seneca's life. He mentions *carmina* (*Annales* XIV 52, 3. *obiciebant etiam eloquentiae laudem uni sibi adsciscere et carmina crebrius factitare, postquam Neroni amor eorum venisset.*) because they can be related as a motive for Nero's jealousy of Seneca, but nothing more specific. R. Syme has suggested in his *Tacitus*, Oxford 1958, 336, that Tacitus' phrase *dicta factaque* in his biography of Petronius, may include a reference to the *Satyricon*, but this is doubtful. Pliny *N.H.* 37, 20: *T. Petronius consularis moriturus invidia Neronis, ut mensam eius exheredaret, trullam myrrhinam HS CCC emptam fregit.*

[14] A consensus of views now places the *Satyricon* in the time of Nero. The late K. F. C. Rose has argued strongly for a date of composition late in Petronius' life span (as near as possible to 65 A. D.) in "The Date of the Satyricon" *Classical Quarterly* NS XIII, 1, 1962, 166–8; also his "Time and Place in the *Satyricon*," *Transactions of the American Philological Association* XCIII, 1962, 402–9. A. Collignon, *Étude sur Pétrone*, Paris 1892, 172, 391–5, indicates correspondences between Petronius and Martial which he admits (391) are not conclusive in settling which poet influenced the other, or which preceded in time. E. V. Marmorale places the *Satyricon* after 180 A. D., but is equally dubious about the evidence of priority provided by a comparison of texts of these authors. *La Questione Petroniana*, Bari 1948, 263–40; also, Rose "The Petronian Inquisition, An Auto-da-Fé," *Arion*, 1966, 275–301.

[15] Sidonius Apollinaris, 23, 157: the basis of a theory of P's Massilian origin: C. Cichorius, *Römische Studien*, Berlin 1922: "Petronius und Massilia."

[16] Macrobius, *in somnium Scipionis* I, 2, 8.

Apuleius. Johannes Lydus compares him[17] with satirists like Juvenal and
Turnus. Many grammarians saw him as a quarry of linguistic fossils,
as we may see from the collection of fragments not included in the
Satyricon. The excerpts of the *Satyricon* which we possess, apart from
the *Cena*,[18] were probably made in the Ninth or Tenth centuries A. D.,
and the oldest M. S. that we have is likely to be of Eleventh Century
origin. John of Salisbury seems to have known the story of the "Widow
of Ephesus." The popularity of this story does not presuppose the
popularity of Petronius,[19] yet the *excerpta* of the *Satyricon* seem to have
been popular enough in France and Italy. On the whole, Petronius'
influence upon medieval and modern centuries has been slight in pro-
portion to the striking qualities of his work itself. We find that "Restoration" dramatists of the Seventeenth Century regarded Petronius
himself as an attractive figure for use as a character in their plays.[20]
Editions and commentaries of the *Satyricon* have been frequent from
the late Fifteenth Century,[21] but we hardly find a writer with much
psychological insight into Petronius until J. K. Huysmans.[22]

Pétrone Ingénu

Marcel Proust's way of life came to resemble that of Petronius which
is described especially in Tacitus *Annales* XVI, 18, in that he turned the
night into day![23] We know from biographers that Proust chose not to
emerge either for pleasure or business during the day, and that for
the purposes of his work he was quite prepared to simulate a perpetual
night in a darkly shuttered, corklined study.[24] Even more suggestive

[17] Johannes Lydus, *de magistratibus* I, 41.
[18] A. Rini, *Petronius in Italy*, New York 1937, 1–2.
[19] For the widespread occurrence of related themes: Otto Rank, "Die Matrone
von Ephesus, ein Deutungsversuch der Fabel von der Treulosen Witwe,"
Imago I, 1913, 50–60.
[20] Petronius appears as a commonplace stage villain in Nathaniel Lee's
The Tragedy of Nero (1675). The reign of Nero interested Seventeenth Century
dramatists: Mathew Gwinne's *Nero* (1603); the anonymous *Nero* (1624); Thomas
May's *Julia Agrippina Empress of Rome* (1628).
[21] S. Gaselee, "The Bibliography of Petronius." *Transactions of the Biblio-
graphical Society* vol. 10, London, 1910, 141–233.
[22] *À Rebours*, edit. Paris 1926, 40–42. For Joyce's knowledge of Huysmans'
novel: J. S. Atherton, *The Books at the Wake*, London 1959, 257.
[23] Tac. *Annales* XVI, 18, 1. 2: *De C. Petronio pauca supra repetenda sunt.
nam illi dies per somnum, nox officiis et oblectamentis vitae transigebatur; utque
alios industria, ita hunc ignavia ad famam protulerat, habebaturque non ganeo et
profligator, ut plerique sua haurientium, sed erudito luxu.*
[24] Richard H. Barker, *Marcel Proust, a Biography*, New York 1958, 182.

in comparing the two is the interest in perverted sex[25] which appears in their works, though it is impossible to be completely sure that Petronius was himself involved in its multifarious toils, as was Proust. It has been suggested with some plausibility that Petronius' work reveals a tendency to scopophilia.[26] This may be compared with interpretations given to parts of Proust's novel.[27] In addition a certain quality of personality, a sense of naïveté and innocence in the midst of moral and intellectual complications, and in the face of vice itself, constituted probably both the apparent *simplicitas* of Petronius, and the goodness that was attributed to Proust by his friends.[28]

However, such strands of similarity are entangled with the difficulty that Proust's work is full and lengthy, whereas Petronius' book is available only as a set of excerpts. Thus Petronius' work never has a final form, is always fluid, and is perhaps too easily amenable to comparison. That is one aspect of the question. Another, however, is the uniformity of texture that is to be found in all the excerpts: I do not mean a uniformity of style or language, but a characteristic posture on the part of the author towards the presentation of his characters and an original use of language to express this.[29] His characters stand at a special "angle" to the words that they use, and are used of them. Language is used with the sinuousness of reminiscent thought, moulded to suggest an associative autonomic flow, formalised to suggest informality. This may be compared to the impression which Proust's use of language creates in the reader, and if nothing survived but a set of excerpts from his novel, the impression would not be altered, nor would our view of his attitudes be radically changed, though the "flow" of the story would only be intermittently available. Neither author provides examples of the "interior monologue" technique in its purest

[25] G. D. Painter, *Marcel Proust a Biography*, Vol. II London 1965, *passim:* the conversation reported between Proust and Gide (313) has something of the flavour of Petronian naïveté.

[26] Sullivan, Ch. VII, also "The Satiricon of Petronius, Some Psychoanalytical Considerations," *American Imago* 18, 4, 1961. 352–369.

[27] The episode in which Françoise intrudes upon "Albertine" and "Marcel": *Cf.* J. P. Sullivan, "The Satiricon of Petronius, Some Psychoanalytical Considerations." *American Imago* Vol. 18, 4, 1961, 353 369. esp. 361.

[28] Painter II 362–3, Lauris (on seeing Proust dead): "never was so much goodness accompanied by so much intelligence."

[29] This is exclusive of the question of how much vulgar or colloquial usage may occur in the *Satyricon*: (see W. Suess, *De eo quem dicunt inesse Trimalchionis Cenae vulgari sermone*. Dorpat 1926).

unmodified, immediate form,[30] as the direct presentation of the content of a character's thoughts. This occurs in famous passages of *Ulysses*, which were influenced, as Joyce himself claimed, by Edouard Dujardin.[31] But the method and the term are both flexible enough to cover a wide selection of modes of presenting a character's thoughts. Dujardin himself refers to Browning and Dostoievsky as his predecessors in the genre.[32]

Both Petronius and Proust were parodists, and this they share with Joyce.[33] Parody is the physic of a literary age, and in order to flourish it needs a fairly developed literature. Proust assures us that its purgative effect is salutary, and that it can be a homoeopathic cure for a writer of his excessive admiration of some other writer's style. In common with some other remedies, it can exhaust whoever indulges in it to excess, and parodists may be led into an obsessive course of devoting too much of their energies into parody, instead of concentrating on their own proper works.[34] Parody can also involve considerable but not necessarily obvious hostility to its model, and can be outright satire, like the parodies in Petronius, or Hipponax's allusions to Homeric lines.[35]

Parody constitutes an attack upon literary types and forms by representing their main features as closely and clearly as possible. It is useless if it is not recognised as parody, and if it does not sufficiently resemble its target. Not surprisingly, it is at times associated with the breaking of a literary boundary, and the overflow of literary creation into a new form, which is sometimes, at first, regarded as monstrous. Petronius and Joyce parodied and travested the *Odyssey* in the overall frame of their works.[36] More minutely, both used parody in the interior of their works themselves. Petronius parodies Greek romances

[30] Depending upon the *Ulysses* but less elaborately worked, and consequently more immediate is the passage in Thomas Wolfe's *Look Homeward Angel*, 1929, which describes W. O. Gant's thoughts on returning home after a period of wandering in the West of the United States.

[31] R. Ellmann, *James Joyce*, New York 1959, 534–5.

E. Dujardin, *Le monologue intérieur*, Paris 1931, 22–3, speculates on Browning and Dostoievsky as predecessors and inventors in this medium, and adduces the analogy of cinematic techniques: 47–8.

[33] Painter II Ch. 5.

[34] Painter II Ch. 99.

[35] P. Brandt; *Parodorum Epicorum Graecorum*, Lips. 1888; P. Maas, *s.v.* Parodos in *R.E.*; Schmid-Stählin, *Griechische Literaturgeschichte*, I, i, 227, 401, 642, 644.

[36] Killeen 199; W. B. Stanford, *The Ulysses Theme* Oxford 1962; H. Kenner, *Dublin's Joyce*, London 1955, 182.

(probably) Virgil, Lucan, Publilius Syrus, Seneca, and many classical authors.[37] Proust wrote brilliant parodies in a series so protracted that his friends began to fear for his literary repute as a serious writer. In *À la Recherche du Temps Perdu* he inserted the famous Goncourt parody.[38] Joyce parodies advertisements[39] (as Petronius parodies inscriptions), but Joyce's "oxen of the sun" passage is a monumental "phylogenic" parody that ranges through the whole literary tradition that he knew.[40] Proust's novel, Joyce's *Ulysses*, Petronius' *Satyricon*, were startlingly new forms when they appeared. Proust and Joyce have had assiduous literary heirs. Petronius, as far as we can see, had not. In Proust and Joyce, parody transcends its prior limitations and transforms itself into a mode of pure *mimesis*. We cannot be sure that Petronius' parody was in this class, though the originality of the *Satyricon* was in its time of an order comparable with the innovations of *À la Recherche du Temps Perdu* and *Ulysses*. The work freed Petronius from the tyranny of school rhetoric and its styles,[41] but we have not enough of him to tell whether his parody was an internal as well as a technical liberation.

"The Virginal Kip-ranger."[42]

When James Joyce was young, translations of Petronius, if not in vogue, were at least frequent.[43] Oliver St. John Gogarty, Joyce's friend, expressed envy of Petronius in verse which celebrates – none too happily – the Roman author's capacity to use the night as if it were day,[44] and to win fame through indolence. Gogarty was not idle,

---

[37] For authors alluded to in the Satyricon: A. Rini 159; *cf.* E. Courtney, "Parody and Literary Allusion in Menippean Satire," *Philologus* 101 1/2 1962, 86–100.

[38] See Painter's comments *op. cit.* II 102–3.

[39] *Ulysses, passim*, but especially the so-called *Aeolus* passage, and throughout *Finnegans Wake* e.g. 172. 5 "Johns is a different butcher. Next place you are up town pay him a visit etc."

[40] S. Gilbert, *James Joyce's Ulysses*, London 1930, 189–305. R. Ellmann, *James Joyce*, New York 1959, 489–90.

[41] *num alio genere furiarum declamatores inquietantur, qui clamant: "haec vulnera pro libertate publica excepi, hunc oculum pro vobis impendi; date mihi (ducem) qui me ducat ad liberos meos, nam succisi poplites membra non sustinent?" haec ipsa tolerabilia essent, si ad eloquentium ituris viam facerent, nunc et rerum tumore et sententiarum vanissimo strepitu hoc tantum proficiunt, ut cum in forum venerint, putent se in alium orbem terrarum delatos: Satyricon* 1.

[42] Stanislaus Joyce, *My Brothers' Keeper*, London 1958, 160.

[43] Killeen, 194.

[44] Oliver St. John Gogarty, *The Collected Poems*, London 1951, 195.

and however much he roamed the town at night with his cronies, he was not a creature of the night like Proust, Petronius, or Joyce. He was an outgoing, athletic, garrulous, "Attic" or "Ionian" type of Dubliner. Joyce saw him as an Eighteenth Century "buck," but he also discerned in him, perhaps wrongly, an Ulyssean wiliness.[45] He was also a devoted Hellenist.

Like Proust's work, *Ulysses* is a tissue of consciousnesses in which experience of the present blends with reminiscence. It emphasises classic continuity, does not bend time outwards, like Proust's novel, but inwards, making an epic into a day's desultory business. We can tell little about Petronius' attitude to time. Tacitus records Petronius' disregard of the night and day division, which may have no far-reaching implication for his work: it is difficult to see, for instance, what importance Proust's own nocturnal habits may have had for his treatment of time. In Petronius' case, perhaps we may infer something from the two dinner parties in the Cena? The incompleteness of the M.S.S. forbids us to be more precise, and there was a general disregard of time in the Hellenistic novels. Something may be said for the view that the very fragmentation of the work conveys an intensified sense of the "timelessness" that we can see in its longer passages.

In discussing similarities between the *Satyricon* and the *Ulysses*, Dr. J. F. Killeen proposes that Joyce may have drawn upon the *Satyricon* as the inspiration for his own parody of *epos*.[46] This is a more colourful hypothesis than that which W. B Stanford has succeeded in establishing, namely that Joyce must have read Lamb's *Adventures of Ulysses* as part of his school curriculum.[47] However, the hypothesis of Petronian influence is based upon mainly "atmospheric" evidence. Killeen has shown that there was considerable interest in Petronius – poems written about him, translations published – in the last decade of the Nineteenth Century and the first few years of the present one.

[44] (*continued*)   Proconsul of Bithynia
Who loved to turn the night to day
Yet for your ease had more to show
than others for their push and go
Teach us to save spirit's expense
And win to fame through indolence.

[45] As the name 'Buck Mulligan" in Joyce's *Ulysses* itself testifies, Joyce saw Gogarty as resembling the Eighteenth Century Anglo-Irish "Buck" (such as Buck Whaley): Ulick O'Connor, *Oliver St. John Gogarty A Poet and his Times*, London 1964, 38.

[46] Killeen 199, 198–203.

[47] Stanford, *Ulysses Theme* 213; "Ulyssean Qualities in Leopold Bloom," *Comparative Literature* 5, 1953, 125-136, esp. 126.

It is significant too, that some of these appeared in Ireland. We have noted that Oliver Gogarty was interested in Petronius. Tom Kettle, an acquaintance of Joyce, was the author of a poem about Petronius.[48] We might recall also that Arthur Griffith's paper, *United Irishman*, attacked J. M. Synge's "The Shadow of the Glen," on the grounds that it resembled the story of the "Widow of Ephesus," which was regarded as an effusion of Roman decadence.[49] None of this however, forges a straight link between Petronius and Joyce; we know that Joyce knew enough Latin to read Petronius; we do not know that he ever read him.

Killeen may be on firmer ground when he refers to French authors such as Flaubert and Huysmans, both of whom refer to Petronius. Joyce knew these author's works; how intimately, it would be impossible to say – but he certainly knew them.[50] This does not discount Killeen's hypothesis in principle: we know from other fields how inventions and new ideas can travel great distances without literary rails on which to run.[51] We cannot be sure that comparable attitudes, uses of language, and the like, are not caused by unobserved environmental and personal influences, rather than by literary contact. We cannot deny the possibility that an atmosphere likely to encourage an interest in Petronius, such as that of the last decade of the Nineteenth Century, might well influence the growth of characteristics that seemed to be Petronian, in some writer who himself had little knowledge of Petronius.

Let us look for example at a personal characteristic that Petronius and Joyce seem to have in common. This is the quality of detachment, the submergence of the satirical or romantic persona of the author.[52]

---

[48] Killeen 194.

[49] J. M. Synge's "The Shadow of the Glen" was strongly criticised in Arthur Griffith's *United Irishman* Oct. 17th, 1903, for representing a version of a story of Roman decadence based on Petronius. In a history of the controversy: D. H. Greene, "The Shadow of the Glen and the Widow of Ephesus" *PMLA* 1947-238, indicates wider influences upon Synge's play. Further, see Otto Rank, note 19 above.

[50] Ellmann, 78-9; Atherton 257; *Finnegans Wake* 346–8.

[51] "Tibet, India and Malaya as sources of Medieval Western Technology," Lynn White Jr. *American Historical Review* LXV, 3, 1960, 515–26: Slaves and other less identifiable media conveyed important inventions to the west · he concluded (526): "despite difficult communication, Mankind in the Old World at least has long lived in a more uniform realm of discourse than we have been prepared to admit."

[52] Killeen 201; Ellmann 142–3, quoting from Stanislaus Joyce's Diary: "He has a distressing habit of saying quietly to those with whom he is familiar the most shocking things about himself and others." *Cf.* note 53 below.

The role of artist is more important to each of them than the role of author. They are not particular about the world's opinion of their personalities; consider Petronius' *neglegentia sui*,[53] and his outrageous self-denigrating remarks, and Joyce's "nail-paring" indifference.[54] Killeen is right to regard neither of them as moralists,[55] though it is not at all remarkable that some have seen in Petronius a fine example of Epicurean *ataraxia*[56] and in Joyce a principal moral satirist of this age. Neither of them could escape completely from the philosophically framed backgrounds of their early training[57]. If it is philosophical to reject background ideology and the assumptions of society, both are philosophers, but not with intent.

In their styles of writing, both rejected current and accepted attitudes. Petronius attacked the dead rhetoric of his time;[58] Joyce exhibits a knowledgeable distaste for the dead rhetoric of a dead capital which he yet must use.[59] Both deploy the vulgar rhetoric that they disliked, together with the colloquial usages of ordinary talk to transcend literary customs and escape current mannerisms in which they could see no future.

There can be discerned in common between them a personal trait of innocence and simplicity which could hardly be credited by their contemporaries in the light of their apparent corruption. Somehow, careless though they were of repute, they remained untouched by what

---

[53] Tac. *Annales* XVI, 18, 2: *ac dicta factaque eius quanto solutiora et quandem sui neglegentiam praeferentia, tanto gratius in speciem simplicitatis accipiebantur.*

[54] In: *A Portrait of the Artist*: Killeen 201.

[55] Killeen 201.

[56] G. Highet "Petronius the Moralist," *Transactions of the American Philological Association* 72, 1941, 176–194; O. Raith, *Petronius ein Epikureer*, Diss. Erlangen 1963. J. P. Sullivan, "Petronius, Artist or Moralist?" *Arion* VI, 1. 1967, 71–87; Syme 553.

[57] W. Noon, *Joyce and Aquinas*, Yale 1957; Raith: *op. cit.*

[58] *Satyricon* 1–3.

[59] *Cf.* Joyce's use of the "dead" but still persistent "classical" tradition or rhetoric in Dublin: Hugh Kenner argues that Joyce parodies this tradition at the same time as he uses it: *Dublin's Joyce*, London 1955, 16: "There is no directness in Dublin; no Parnell now acts out of middle-heart; the great orators are dead, the live ones degraded. Every phase of thought and action has a received analogue or a bookish correspondence. So Joyce's task was to take account of the patterns that lie just outside of the corporeal citizen and his empirical city. He solved it by being as indirect as they, coming at them by means of their analogues, parodying the models according to which they behaved, his attention focused on the invisible point of coincidence between half-living people and half-real literature, opera, oratory, and music." *Cf.* 214, where Kenner connects Bloom with Cicero *Cf.* also (especially) the first three chapters of the surviving *Satyricon*, on which this passage makes fine commentary.

they have done or seen. Our cliché about "artistic" integrity may serve to describe what this quality might have been, but it remains difficult to tie up in a satisfactorily neat definition. This "purity" of the devoted artist enabled Petronius to do what he pleased and say what he pleased, just as unrestrainedly and certainly less self-consciously than any Cynic philosopher of the First Century A. D.[60] It permitted Joyce to haunt Dublin's old brothel quarter without apparent effect upon the light, joyous temper of his youth. Gogarty did not call him the "virginal kip -ranger" for nothing.[61]

Petronius, like Joyce and like Proust, broke through the accepted boundaries of contemporary art forms to produce something distinctive and new.[62] All of them present human nature with detailed sensibility; thoughts and feelings are made available more immediately to the reader or listener than is the case in conventional narrative or even in drama. The form is less obtrusive, and is almost submerged in the content. No doubt Joyce went much further along these lines than Petronius, and in his later work his conflation of form and content (distinct categories both to the ancients and the Latinate Joyce) was almost ostentatious. Joyce's early "non serviam"[63] was maintained in later life: he would serve no society or set of assumptions in which he did not believe, and he withdrew into intense privacy which his bardic blindness accentuated. Proust and Petronius isolated themselves, as it were, at the centre of the whirlwind, and their form of alienation from society at large and ordinary life, was simply to remain ensconced in fashionable "Society". Joyce's "exile silence and cunning,"[64] were perhaps more realistic means of procuring safety from stimuli arising from involvement in human society and its consequential claims upon his sym-

---

[60] H. D. Rankin, "On Tacitus' Biography of Petronius" *Classica et Mediaevalia* XXVI, 1–2 1965 233–45.

[61] S. Joyce. *op cit*. 160–1.

> "There is a young fellow named Joyce
> Who possesses a sweet tenor voice.
> He goes down to the kips
> With a psalm on his lips
> And biddeth the harlots rejoice."

[62] Gellie, *op. cit.*

[63] *A Portrait of the Artist as a Young Man*, London 1930, "Traveller's Library" Edit. 133, 281; H. Gorman, *James Joyce*, New York 1939, 110. Viking Press Edit. 117, 297.

[64] *A Portrait of the Artist as a Young Man*, 281; Ellman 365, points out that the proverb was borrowed from the *Fuge - Late - Tace* of one of Balzac's characters in *Splendeurs et Misères des Courtisanes*.

pathy which would have produced an agonising diversion from the pursuit of art.

> "The very rich who are different from you and me"
>
> Scott Fitzgerald, *The Rich Boy* 1962

Scott Fitzgerald was different from the writers whom we have discussed, both in his relation to literature and his way of life. He too sought refuge in exile at the centre of society. Some of his work is reminiscent of the social criticism in the *Satyricon* and of its description of certain conditions of society. His concern was more direct than that of Petronius or the others, and he was more conscious of Petronius than the others. We may see in Paul MacKendrick's analysis of *The Great Gatsby* and Trimalchio,[65] how Fitzgerald found in Petronius' work examples of the life led in the midst of a materialistic nightmare of the "Twenties." It is well known, for instance, that Fitzgerald originally had intended to call *The Great Gatsby* by the name *Trimalchio at West Egg*. Fitzgerald saw exemplified in Trimalchio the symptom of a sick society; *Gatsby* exemplified the sicknesses of the Twenties: conspicuous consumption, shallow culture, immense wealth. The tendency of MacKendrick's argument is that Petronius might have been, as Fitzgerald was, an outsider[66] in the group of the enormously wealthy and powerful, – one who perceived their sublime incomprehension of the human status and dignity of these who were outside their group. They would, however, partially accept an artist if he had taken pains to acquire the protective colouration of their mannerisms. It was a dangerous course for the artist to pursue: the rich could take up a man of talent, consume him for amusement, fancy, or convenience, and then toss him aside. Fitzgerald knew how very different in power and prestige such people were from himself, and he resented it: he resented the easy way they took the prizes, especially the prize of love.[67] It was unfortunate for him that, after an early setback, he should have seemed to beat them in this sphere, only to acquire a relationship that had much tragedy in it.[68]

[65] Paul MacKendrick, "The Great Gatsby and Trimalchio," *Classical Journal* 45, 7, 1950, 307–14.

[66] MacKendrick 313; Petronius' detachment is sufficiently indicated in Tacitus' *Annales* XVI, 18–20.

[67] MacKendrick, 314.

[68] MacKendrick, 312: "For Gatsby is Fitzgerald, and the novel is a condition contrary to fact in past time – Gatsby's story might have been Fitzgerald's if *This side of Paradise* had not made the author enough money to marry Zelda Sayre."

Petronius was destroyed by the monster of wealth and power, though not, as far as we know, by any of its agents in the form of love. It was probably his intellectual brilliance and consequent court influence that provoked the hatred of Tigellinus, who represented him to Nero as a traitor. He was destroyed, if you like, by his professional rival as court-entertainer. He had to be brilliant to live where he lived, and he had to conceal it in order to go on living. The intellectual hides himself from the tyrant with whom he nevertheless lives.[69] Once aroused by Tigellinus, Nero's cruel suspicion was unappeasable; so also was his paranoid tendency to turn upon his friends.

Petronius was forced to die. It is to his credit, and equally a felicitous example of his art, that he died mocking both the pleasures and the philosophies of the society in which he had chosen to live, and bitterly ridiculed its arch-representative, Nero. Petronius' death illustrates his peculiar brand of detachment,[70] and it is perhaps a feasible interpretation of Tacitus' narrative to say that Petronius knew that he needed the monstrosity of Roman society for his art, but knew that he needed it for no other purpose.

I incline to disagree with MacKendrick's view that Petronius has created in Trimalchio a figure that is parallel with the monomaniac Gatsby.[71] Neither Trimalchio nor Gatsby belong to the class of the sinisterly cool rich who are "different from you and me." Trimalchio is not all satire: there is rudimentary common sense embedded in his absurdities, which, significantly, are part of his apparatus of social pretension, and are sometimes cast off. He regards his slaves as human beings,[72] remembering no doubt his own slave origins, and when he asks "What is a poor man?"[73] it is not Trimalchio who is alone in being satirized, nor even the schools of rhetoric; it is all society. He is a

---

[69] "A system where the richest man gets the most beautiful girl if he wants her, where the artist without an income has to sell his talents to a butter manufacturer," quoted from *This Side of Paradise*; MacKendrick 312: *Cf.* TennesseeWilliams *Camino Real* (Block 6) where Kilroy is forced by Gutman to accept employment as a "Patsy."

[70] Tac. *Annales* XVI, 19, 1–3: *nec tulit ultra timoris aut spei moras. neque tamen praeceps vitam expulit, sed incisas venas, ut libitum, obligatas aperire rursum et adloqui amicos, non per seria aut quibus gloriam constantiae peteret. audiebatque referentis nihil de immortalitate animae et sapientium placitis, sed levia carmina et faciles versus.*

[71] Possibly "Gatsby" is a "significant" name suggesting "son of a gun" *terrae filius*? It would suit his "epic" character.

[72] 71, 1: *et servi homines sunt et aeque unum lactem biberunt, etiam si illos malus fatus oppresserit.*

[73] 48, 5: *quid est pauper?*

natural person, as Petronius implies,[74] and is treated in the *Satyricon* with a blunt amusement which is very different from the slow, accurate flaying that Fitzgerald inflicts upon his rich characters. In the *Cena*, Trimalchio threatens much evil, but commits little. The rich people in *The Great Gatsby* are in fact careless and destructive of outsiders, not unlike the rich *piscinarii* of the late Republic.[75] In Gatsby there subsists a strand of naïve and simple honesty, and in a sense he is much more naïve than Trimalchio.[76] Gatsby committed crimes which are left to our imagination in order to win the love of a girl whom he loved in a simple, adolescent, Romantic way. He is much more innocent, and indeed more "pure" than the Buchanans whose friendship brings him to his death. Trimalchio, however, is a man whose life has been a rough-and-tumble of action and ambition. He has made money, and is enjoying it in his old age. He will have a most respectable, in fact, luxurious funeral, and is looking forward to it with intense liveliness – so much that he has to act it out in mime at his party.[77] This death-orientation could hardly be called morbid.[78] He began his career as a slave and prostituted himself to his owners.[79] He implies that he was sensible to do this voluntarily, and to make the best that he could of the situation. His owner left him money, which was the beginning of his success.[80]

He is essentially a simple character, a dedicated boaster, a man who takes his pleasures and admits his own misdeeds with a candour that is almost Homeric. No sense of shame dogs him, but he has an explosive temper which he indulges moderately enough considering how ample is his liberty to do so. So far from being different from his fellows, Trimalchio seems to have much in common with the freedmen guests at his dinner, some of whom, at least, he must be financing.[81] His only apparent

---

[74] 52, 10–11; *Cf.* 37, 4–8.

[75] Cicero *ad Atticium* II 1. 7; Syme, *The Roman Revolution*, Oxford 1939, 44–5; 162–75.

[76] MacKendrick 310: "he 'Gatsby' devoted his whole corrupt life to the realising of his uncorruptible dream."

[77] 78, 5–6.

[78] Since he does not accept the notion of death at all: 78, 3–4, *statim ampullam nardi aperuit omnesque nos unxit et "spero" inquit "futurum ut aeque me mortuum iuvet tamquam vivum";* for a different view: W. Arrowsmith, "Luxury and Death in the Satyricon," *Arion* V. 3, 1966, 304–31.

[79] 75, 11.

[80] 76, 2.

[81] 76, 10.

difference is that he is richer than they,[82] and it is possible to imagine him at the early stage of his career in which we observe them as they converse at the *Cena*. He has a certain humorous awareness of the transformation of his fortunes, and he is not cruelly arrogant, though he is undoubtedly vulgar.

"Trimalchian" simplicity is very different from the *species simplicitatis* which is attributed to Petronius himself by Tacitus.[83] This simplicity of Trimalchio is real and not a mask, no mere *species*. In Proust, Joyce,[84] (and to a lesser degree Fitzgerald) the simplicity of *persona* which they present is based upon a genuine psychological characteristic, but it is coexistent with intellectual and artistic complexity. It is not unreasonable, and it is certainly tempting, to imagine that Petronius was like this. To put it another way, the possession of a naïve wit does not entail naïveté, but in some surroundings the intellectual is forced to be apparently naïve, an apparently good fellow, with no eccentricities and paradoxes. Or, if he has such, they are too absurd for serious consideration. This does not detract from the simplicity of tone and manner given to a personality by some overriding preoccupation, such as art, or religion, scientific research, or even the conscientious pursuit of selfish ends.[85]

Scott Fitzgerald shares with Petronius this "apparent" simplicity in a marked way. To survive socially in the group in which he wished to live, he had to conceal his analytic, critical and essentially subversive attitude to the social dispensation which allowed his rich friends to flourish in overpowering luxury. So well did he succeed in concealing his own self from the superficial gaze of the public, that he earned the reputation of a socialite, a camp-follower of the rich, a journalist

[82] *Cf*. Ernest Hemingway's comment on the notion of the "very rich who are different from you and me" – "Yes, they have more money," — a response which hits off the attitudes of Trimalchio and his friends.

[83] This *simplicitas* was an assumed *persona* of old-fashioned simplicity, an archaic good quality; H. Stubbe, *Philologus* suppl. 25, 150–1. H. Bogner, *Hermes* 1941, 223–4; E. Bickel, *Rheinisches Museum* XC, 1941, 269–72.

[84] Ezra Pound expresses this attitude of majestic simplicity very well: Canto XXVII, 1.
"An" that year, Metevesky went over to America
del Sud (and the Pope's manners were so like Mr Joyce's
got that way in the Vatican, weren't like that before)"
Joyce's artistic *persona* is not firmly in place in his letters to his wife from Dublin in 1909, which range from hysteria to ecstacy in their tone: *Letters of James Joyce*, edit. Ellmann, London 1966: Vol. II.

[85] e.g. the mixture of evil and charm in Catilina, as remarked by Cicero, *Pro Caelio* 12–13.

of their expensive doings. So far from being a sycophantic chronicler of conspicuous waste, his earlier works were in a distinct sense a parody of the "social" writer. His immediate aspect, like that of Petronius, was deceptive. He seemed to be (like Petronius, he had to seem to be) what he was not.

Where there is a multitude of stimuli, a multiplicity of opportunities for experience, simplicity in style of living can be a convenient defence against madness and destruction, and in this respect the simplicity of the king and the apparent simplicity of the court jester can confront each other. It is the only way in which they can. But the jester cannot let his mask drop, or like Petronius, he is destroyed. He can hint, and this is what both Petronius and Fitzgerald had to do.

Fitzgerald understood that the appearance of civilised simplicity is in most cases dearly bought. Much scholarly discussion has tried to elucidate what the *simplicitas* of Tacitus' phrase *in speciem simplicitatis* (*Ann.* XVI, 18, 3, note 53 above) means. Fitzgerald has a passage in "Tender is the Night" which seems to constitute a most telling comment upon this phrase, and upon the atmosphere of Tacitus' biography of Petronius.

The circumstances are: Dick Diver, a principal character in Fitzgerald's novel, appears on the beach in a pair of bathing trunks which appear to be made of nothing but black lace, but which in fact have a lining of pink material, which has been calmly and laboriously stitched in by his wife. He is duly ridiculed for this "pansy's trick" by the bystanders ,but the ingénue Rosemary is very much amused by it. Fitzgerald writes:[86]

"Her naïveté responded wholeheartedly to the expensive simplicity of the Divers', unaware of its complexity and its lack of innocence, unaware that it was a selection of quality rather than quantity from the world's bazaar, and that simplicity of behaviour also, the nursery-like peace and goodwill, the emphasis on the simpler virtues, was part of a desperate bargain with the gods, and had been attained through struggles she could not have guessed at. At that moment, the Divers represented externally the exact furthermost evolution of a class, so that most people seemed awkward beside them, in reality a qualitative change had set in that was not at all apparent to Rosemary."

Here, it seems, we have the illustration of two kinds of "simplicity." The Divers' simplicity is the "apparent" simplicity of Petronius,

[86] *Tender is the Night*: Bodley Head edit. Vol. II London 1959, 91.

Rosemary's is like that of Trimalchio, it accepts the apparent standards of a society that in its most advanced cultural core has moved away from these standards. Nobody knew better than Petronius what was elegant, for it was people like himself who created taste. So too did the Divers in Fitzgerald's novel.

No doubt we might be inclined to see in each of the writers whom we have discussed in relation to Petronius, some common ground in the apparent naïveté and simplicity in their own lives and in the impression created by some parts of their works. But this aspect of them is contingent upon their own basic attitudes to the societies in which they lived, and ultimately upon their views of the human condition. Each of them was expressing in his own fashion a distinct individuality; they were critical, indeed hostile to many aspects of the society in which they found themselves. This is not to say that any of them was a moralist. It was sufficiently difficult to be an artist, indeed more difficult, since what the artist says often comes more closely home to the innermost feelings of his audience than does the philosophising of the moralist. The point about all of them that comes out clearly is that they were individualists in a mode that was different from the outspoken hostility to society's ways that is to be found in an ancient Cynic's παρρησία or *libertas*, or in the outright strictures of a modern reformer or propagandist. Also they reflected and registered social phenomena rather than attempted to initiate them. A further point is that they all had conspicuous personal troubles: Petronius' final moment of truth in which he wrote down Nero's vices in his will, may not mean more than that he hated Nero, but this, if true, is still something important.[87] His picture of anomic life in Italy projects a greater discontent than his final outburst, taken alone, suggests, – even if we do not go so far as to identify him with Encolpius.[88] Proust was separated from society by asthma and homosexuality, and lived by night, a significant and active comment on how life was lived in his time. Joyce's myth-making was beset in its progress by his blindness, and by drink, and also, as is most apparent in some early letters to his wife, by a profound neurosis on the question of friendship, marital love and trust, all of which are well aired in *Ulysses*.[89] It is interesting

[87] It is not easy to agree with Sullivan, 257, that there is no evidence of Petronius' discontent with Nero's court, or of *Angst*: both the biography of P. in Tacitus, and the *Satyricon* itself seem to imply something different.

[88] Sullivan's theory (note 26 above) entails some identification of Petronius with Encolpius.

[89] Joyce's letters to his wife : note 84 above.

to note that both Joyce and Petronius had misgivings about friendship,[90] if we can take the picture of betrayed friendship in the *Satyricon* as meaning much. Proust doubted whether friendship was possible.[91] Scott Fitzgerald suffered from marital insecurity and sought alienation in alcohol.[92] Like Joyce, he struggled manfully under the burden of his familial and personal responsibilities and problems for a number of years. No wonder that they donned their respective forms of simplicity.

In a society which preserves a long literary tradition as an element in its education, the influence of an author can stretch for many centuries. Homer is still immediate, is frequently translated, and was a source of motivation and an origin of structure for one of the most remarkable works of this century. Themes from the *epos* well up as comments upon the perpetual human tragedy, and will do so, presumably, as long as memory of *epos* lasts. What happened in *Ulysses* happened in the *Satyricon;* writers who were sated with the complexity of the immediate tradition decided to delve deeper into the literary history of their cultures; to seek genuine metal for their own constructions. Writers of this century, such as Joyce, Proust, Fitzgerald are within the ambit of Petronian influence, directly or indirectly, and further, give indications in their lives and works, of "Petronian" responses. The response to anomie in society at large is clear: it is opposed by the writer clinging to his art as to a religion, and presenting minutely what he sees. By meticulous industry and artistic dedication, he keeps the wolf of anomie from the door for a while. There is something loosely textured in the characters that they present, a fluidity, a lack of wholeness. Some Homeric heroes show this same looseness and lability. Encolpius is nearer to Achilles or Agamemnon than we might care to think: Odysseus is different, and quite untypical of his heroic social context.[93] He wins his battle against life's pressures without placing too high a value on his victory.

---

[90] Ellmann, 120–1.

[91] See the list of themes under this heading: P. A. Spalding, *A Reader's Handbook to Proust*, London 1952, 170–1; Petronius' doubts about the validity of human friendship are well expressed in the verses of *Satyricon*, 80.

[92] On Fitzgerald's sense of sexual inadequacy and anxiety: E. Hemingway, *A Moveable Feast*, London 1964, chs. 17, 18, 19, esp. p. 171. F's "classical" pessimism is well expressed in a letter to his daughter (1936): "I feel it is your duty to accept the tragedy, the sadness of the world we live in, with a certain *esprit.*"

[93] Stanford, *Ulysses Theme*, 67.

The standing of these modern writers is high. There is, however, a distinct critical tendency to place Petronius in the second rank.[94] In this can be seen the still living influence of a critical tradition that stems from Cicero and Quintilian. At all events, if Petronius' influence is what it seems to be, his abortive revolt against the decaying monolith of rhetoric has had vivid, albeit long delayed, consequences in our time.

[94] Averbach, *op. cit.*, Sullivan, 261–9.

ON TACITUS' BIOGRAPHY OF PETRONIUS

Our most important authority for the life of Petronius is Tacitus. There is no longer any serious doubt that the writer of the *Satyricon* is the same man as that whom Tacitus described with such attention and vividness in Book XVI, chapters 17 and 18 (19, 20) of the *Annales*.[1] The purpose of this essay is to examine Tacitus' account of Petronius, and to reassess it, considering first of all Tacitus' attitude to Petronius in the light of the factors which probably moulded it, and secondly the philosophical affinities of Petronius and of Tacitus' source of information about him.

Let us recapitulate Tacitus' account: in chapter 17, he records a list of people who were killed in 66 A.D. in the prolonged reign of terror that was triggered off by the conspiracy of Piso.[2] The background of these deaths needs little gloss: the terror had got so far out of hand that private enmity was able to take advantage of public hysteria. The equestrian order came in for its share of the killings, and Tacitus bleakly lists the names of the casualties without detail or comment. Among these names is a certain Petronius (praenomen uncertain)[3].

---

[1] H. Furneaux, *Cornelii Taciti Annalium ab Excessu Divi Augusti Libri*, Oxford 1891, Vol. II, notes on XVI 18; Kroll, *Realencyclopaedie s.v.* Petronius, 1202; Schanz-Hosius, *Römische Literaturgeschichte*, Teil II 509–520. There is now a general acceptance of the identity of the Petronius in Tacitus' *Annales* with the author of the Satyricon. *Cf.* R. Syme, *Tacitus*, Oxford 1958, 336, 548.

[2] For a collection of references to Piso in Tacitus' text, see P. Fabia, *Onomasticon Taciteum*, Paris/Lyon 1900, 535–6. *Cambridge Ancient History* Vol. X, 726 ff.

[3] There is doubt about this praenomen; whether it is represented by a C or T in Tacitus' text it is almost impossible to decide definitely: Furneaux, *op. cit.*; Kroll, *op. cit.*, Petronius Arbiter is the name in the M.S.S.: Τίτος Πετρώνιος in Plutarch's essay on "How to discern a flatterer from a true friend."

In chapter 18 Tacitus introduces a digression about this man Petronius, somewhat self-consciously (*De (C) Petronio, pauca repetenda sunt*). Then, immediately, he suggests as sufficient reason for his digression, the strangeness of Petronius' way of life: *nam illi dies per somnum, nox officiis et oblectamentis vitae transigebatur etc.* We are told that *ignavia* brought Petronius fame, just as *industria* did for others.[4] He was not regarded as a rascal and a wastrel, like most of those who spent their property, but as an expert on luxury (*erudito luxu*). The more uninhibited his words and actions became, the more enthusiastically they were received as examples of charming naïveté: *ac dicta factaque eius quanto solutiora et quandam sui neglegentiam praeferentia, tanto gratius in speciem simplicitatis accipiebantur.* However, as Proconsul in Bithynia, Petronius showed himself to be both efficient and capable. After this, he relapsed into his vicious ways, or at least appeared to do so (*dein revolutus ad vitia seu vitiorum imitatione*), and was taken up into membership of Nero's intimate circle (*inter paucos familiarium*) as *arbiter elegantiae:* Nero did not consider anything to be chic (*amoenum et molle etc.*) unless Petronius gave it the seal of his approval. Consequently, Petronius provoked the dislike of Tigellinus, who was jealous of his rivalry in the science of pleasure. Tigellinus stimulated Nero's dominant emotion, cruelty, by suggesting that Petronius had been a friend of Scaevinus.[5] A slave was suborned to act as informer; the right of defence was removed, and the greater part of Petronius' household was imprisoned.

Chapter 19 tells us that Nero was on his way to Campania at this time, and that Petronius attempted to follow him, but was held back at Cumae. He realised that he was doomed, and decided to waste no more time on either hope or fear. However, he did not kill himself immediately, but opened his veins and had them closed up again temporarily, so that he could open them once more at his leisure. In the meantime he entertained himself with the conversation of his friends: enjoyed a good dinner, rewarded some of his slaves and pu-

---

[4] Tacitus had a penchant for paradoxical characters of this kind: R. Syme, *op. cit.* 545, implies that this preference has its own perversity: "Tacitus meets out a subversive justice: an equity without benevolence: imparts a uniform and gloomy colouring to the whole picture of life under the Caesars." For his attitude to men who were the moral exemplars of the age: Syme, 336–338, 553.

[5] Fabia, 279–280. Scaevinus had some points of character in common with Petronius: elements in his character which would lend colour to the charges made against him: *Annales* 15, 49: *nam Scaevino dissoluta luxu mens et proinde vita somno languida.*

nished others. He did not spend his time seeking the consolations of philosophy or engaged in serious discourse: he enjoyed light songs and verses. After his dinner he indulged in a slight sleep, in order to make his compelled suicide seem to be as much as possible a natural death. Not only did Petronius differ from Nero's serious philosophical martyrs in respect of his premortuary conversation: he went so far as to parody their custom of giving philosophical lectures on the point of death (like Seneca) or recording testamentary praises and placatory bequests to Nero and Tigellinus to ensure the safety of surviving relatives. He achieved this parody by writing out before his death a systematic account of the emperor's perverse sexual practices, and listed the names of the men and women who were collaborators in them. He sealed this document and sent it to Nero. Then he broke his signet, in case it should be used afterwards to incriminate innocent people.[6]

Chapter 20 takes the story a stage further. It reveals Nero as being puzzled about how the news of his nocturnal amusements had leaked out. A woman called Silia was identified as Petronius' informant. She was the wife of a senator, and of some social consequence. She was a participant in the orgies, and she was also on very friendly terms with Petronius (*perquam familiaris*).[7] She was an expert in all forms of sexual activity. Nero sent her into exile ostensibly because she had not kept silence about what she had seen and done, but really because he disliked her. After this, we have in the next chapter descriptions of the deaths of Thrasea and Soranus.

One of the most striking aspects of this account of Petronius' life is that in respect of moral depravity and the commission of really vicious acts, Petronius' innocence is given the benefit of doubt. This possibly indicates that Tacitus chose to follow favourable views in the literary source or sources which he used and with which, for his own reasons, he was prepared to agree by and large. It indicated that Petronius' contemporaries did not take him seriously as a profligate, though they were prepared to accept him as a jester (*dicta factaque* etc.)[8] They

[6] Pliny, *N. H.* 37, 2 (7, 20) tells a story which is remarkably of a piece with his precautionary act: namely that Petronius before he died, broke a valuable vase that Nero coveted to prevent the emperor from gaining possession of it.

[7] Silia is only mentioned in Tacitus: *perquam familiaris* does not necessarily imply sexual intimacy. A. Gerber et A. Greef, *Lexicon Taciteum*: Lips 1903. *R.E.* Silia (29) Nagl.

[8] Syme 336: suggests that this phrase possibly includes the *Satyricon* which, like [Seneca's] pasquinade on the deification of Claudius, Tacitus does not see fit to mention.

refused to accept the moralist's self-propagated myth that he was an immoral monster. His naïve frankness about his comparatively minor vices was taken to be rather a charming old-fashioned *simplicitas*,[9] for all that it was probably phrased in his own elegant and self-conscious locutions. This account in the source material which Tacitus used, seems to have convinced him of its truth. It is credible enough that it should, for writers who concern themselves with writing the lives of imperial victims are more likely to establish the virtue of their subject, where there is any doubt about his virtue, rather than to suggest that his vice was not to be taken seriously. In fact, Tacitus' narrative has the ring of credibility, just as it reflects his own credence in it, or its sources. Tacitus' conviction of its truthfulness is shown by an interesting turn that he gives to his methodologically formulaic but verbally varied expression of scepticism about people not being what they seem: *dein revolutus ad vitia, seu vitiorum imitatione.* Though Tacitus' assessments along these lines are sometimes more formal than analytical, it is much more usual for him to speak of virtues that may only seem to be virtues; it is not usual for him to speak of vices that may only seem to be vices. We are much more accustomed to the sort of thing that is said of Piso: *Virtutes vel virtutibus similes*, XV, 48.)[10] Tacitus had a careful regard for the public and its *pronis auribus*[11] and scepticism about virtue came more easily to him than incredulity about vice. In short, Tacitus was not the man to invent virtues where there were no grounds

[9] Probably an archaic and distinctly Roman characteristic. H. Stubbe, Die Verseinlagen in Petronius," *Philologus*, suppl. 25 Hft. 2. especially, 150–151, regards the poem of chapter 132 as having a programmatic significance: *quid me constricta spectatis fronte Catones/damnatisque novae simplicitatis opus?* This *simplicitas* possibly was "realism" – according to Stubbe. H. Bogner, *Hermes* 1941, 223–4 examines the few occurrences of the word: *simplicitas* in Tacitus and concludes that no especial meaning can be given to the word in the text, though he considers that Petronius' contemporaries probably regarded it as programmatic. E. Bickel, "Petrons simplicitas bei Tacitus", *Rheinisches Museum* XC, 1941, 269–272, considers that the *simplicitas* of the poem at Ch. 132 is archaic simplicity of ethos, and endeavours to link it with Greek ἀπλότης: Ovid *Met.* 15, 120: *quid meruere boves, animal sine fraude dolisque /innocuum simplex?* *Heroides* 16, 316: *utere mandatis simplicitate viri.*

[10] Tacitus' statement about Petronius would thus be a neat ironic reversal of his favourite theme of apparent virtues concealing substantial vices: *Annales* 15, 48, 6: (Piso) *claro apud vulgum rumore erat per virtutem aut species virtutibus similis. Hist. I 52, 11: aviditate imperii dandi ipsa vitia (Vitelli) pro virtutibus interpretabantur; Hist. I, 71, 4: falsae virtutes* - and many other loci: see article on *species (specie* + genitive) in *Lex. Tac.* 1532.

[11] *obtrectatio et livor pronis auribus accipiuntur: Hist.* I, 1, 11. For the general harshness of Tacitus' attitudes: Syme, *op. cit.*

for believing them to exist. Consequently, the latitude granted by him
to Petronius probably corresponds to a favourable view taken of
Petronius in some source which Tacitus was following. The unfavour-
able references to Petronius may also be from the same source, – representing facts which the author of the source could scarcely conceal.
On the other hand, it is possible that they came from a different source
– which is on the face of it less likely. There is also the possibility that
Tacitus worked them up himself from a general tradition.

It is clear that Tacitus and at least one of his sources do not fully
believe that Petronius was one of Nero's fellow-orgiasts. In the first
instance, if he had been personally involved, then he would not have
needed information from Silia about what went on at these gatherings.
The implication is clear: Nero could not imagine how Petronius could
have been informed about something of which Nero clearly (according
to the narrative) supposed that he was ignorant. The implication is
that Tacitus and/or his source exonerates Petronius from the most
intimate complicity in Nero's vices, and regards him as being more or
less an "outsider." It would be naïve to suppose that if Petronius were
cleared of this suspicion, it would necessarily follow that he was a
chaste and blameless man. Also it would be unreasonable to assume
that simply because he was *ex hypothesi* not a party to these activities
of the emperor, he had never been a party to any such activities. The
exonerating implication may be valid only for the latter part of Petronius' life when he was beginning to fall under a shadow of disfavour as
a result of Tigellinus' propaganda against him. But at least one of
Tacitus' sources is keen to whitewash Petronius, and Tacitus is content enough to agree, though he does not suppress certain contradictory elements which (a) may be from a different source but possibly
belong to the favourable one *per saturam;* (b) appealed in themselves
to Tacitus' personal and at the same time highly stylised awareness of
moral paradox; (c) also appealed to his sceptical Thucydidean-Sallus-
tian historian's pose.

The contradictory elements are clear enough: even on the view that
Petronius had at one time been a member of the innermost circle of
Nero's friends(*inter paucos familiarium*) and was excluded on falling
into disfavour, he could scarcely have needed Silia to tell him about the
vices and the persons involved. The story in Tacitus says that he was
regarded as *elegantiae arbiter*, and there is no implication that the *elegan-
tia* was exclusively concerned with the more decorous arts. There is,
by the same token, no necessity to regard it as entailing sexual depra-

vity. Tacitus' account, however, by its use of Silia, implies that the closeness of Petronius (as *arbiter* etc.) to Nero was more like the closeness of Seneca to Nero, rather than that of Silia. Further, on general grounds, it is reasonable to suppose that Petronius would have heard rumours of Nero's vices and of his collaborators in them from sources other than Silia: we may recall that soldiers like Subrius Flavus were able to tax Nero with being a murderer and matricide.[12] *A fortiori*, it is likely enough that Petronius would be informed by general court rumour about Nero's vices. It looks very much as if Silia is introduced as an explanation of how a man, honest, decent and perhaps moderately chaste, could possibly have known about these matters in detail. Tacitus says that she was ostensibly blamed for divulging information to Petronius, but was exiled *proprio odio*. This was the real reason for her exile, and it is possible that she has been introduced by Tacitus' source into the biography of Petronius in order to whitewash Petronius by means of the suggestion that he needed her as an informant. Nero tended to turn against his close friends sooner or later, especially those who had an intimate knowledge of his personal vices: and it is of course not beyond possibility that Petronius had some real knowledge of them which accelerated the growth of Nero's dislike of him at the instigation of Tigellinus. And if we believe in Tigellinus' dislike, we must surely conclude that the power of Petronius with the emperor was sufficient to make him worth disliking. His hold over the emperor must have been comparable in its strength to that of Tigellinus (and to some degree that of Seneca in his earlier helpless and optimistic connivance[13],) and it was based upon his capacity to suggest pleasures. The suggestion that Petronius was on terms of close friendship with Silia is not in itself incriminating: Cicero had Fulvia as an informant, and yet escaped with his reputation untarnished. Other discrepancies reside in the actual personality of Petronius: the contrast of his *ignavia* and his efficiency; his open speech that almost incriminated himself. These, however, are simply the marks of an original and paradoxical character, and need not represent indulgence in actual vices.

This rather sympathetic treatment which Petronius receives from

[12] Annales XV 67, 2: *"oderam te" inquit, "nec quisquam tibi fidelior militum fuit, dum amari meruisti. Odisse coepi postquam parricida matris et uxoris, auriga et histrio et incendiarus exstitisti."* The impossibility of hoodwinking the public at large is illustrated by the following popular verses recorded by Suetonius, *Nero* 39: *Quis negat Aeneae magna de stirpe Neronem? sustulit hic matrem, sustulit ille patrem* and: Νέρων Ὀρέστης Ἀλκμέων μητροκτόνος.

[13] *Annales*, XV 67–8.

Tacitus could be attributed to Tacitus' regard for a fellow satirist of imperial excess. On the other hand, it seems likely enough, as F. Marx suggests, that Tacitus is following in this section of his work a book which dealt with the lives of Nero's victims, part of the by no means insignificant genre of *"exitus Literatur."*[14] This seems likely enough. The best candidate among the writers of *"exitus"* material is Fannius,[15] who as Pliny tells us (*Ep.* V, 5, 1) left unfinished at his death *pulcherrimum opus* which dealt with the *exitus* of the people killed or exiled by Nero, and which enjoyed considerable popularity. Fannius probably is associated in some way with Fannia,[16] the daughter of Thrasea and Arria. It would be surprising (a): if the tendency of his book was not that to be a victim of Nero was to be presumptively honest and serious (b): if there was no Cynic/Stoic influence colouring the background of his material, considering that there is some evidence that Thrasea at the end of his life held premortuary converse with the Cynic philosopher Demetrius.[17] But it is difficult to form an estimate of Petronius' own philosophical predilections. It has been usual, on suggestive though inconclusive evidence, to regard him as an Epicurean;[18] in fact it is not easy to pin

[14] F. A. Marx, "Tacitus und die Literatur der exitus illustrium virorum," *Philologus*, Bd. XCII, (N. F.) Bd. XLVI. 1937, pp. 83–103.

[15] Marx 83–84; R. E.: Fannius (10); Stein, *Prosopographia Imperii Romani* 116; Schanz-Hosius, Teil II 651; Syme 559.

[16] Fannia (118) *Prosop. Imp. Rom. R. E.* Fannia (22) (Kappelmacher); Arria minor *Prosop. Imp. Rom:* Arria 1114, wife of P. Clodius Thrasea Paetus. R. E. (40) and stemma p. 1259. The entry in *Prosopographia Imperii Romani* on Fannius(116) says: *veri mihi videtur simile eum arta necessitudine coniunctum fuisse cum Fannia filia P. Clodi Thrasea Paeti auctori Nerone damnati eademque uxore Helvidii Prisci qui a Nerone Italia pulsus est* – which seems a most likely connection; also Syme, *op. cit.*

[17] Demetrius was a man of outstanding integrity who was implacably hostile to the principate. *Prosop. Imp. Rom.* Demetrius (39). *R. E. Von Arnim*, Demetrius (91). Überweg-Praechter, *Grundriss der Geschichte der Philosophie* Bd. I. 505; Tac. *Annales* 16, 34–5. (*Thrasea*) *inlustrium virorum feminarumque coetum frequentum egerat maxime intentus Demetrio Cynicae institutionis doceri.* Dio Cassius 66, 11, 13, describes Demetrius' characteristically Cynic abusiveness towards Vespasian, whose response is said to have been along the lines: σὺ μὲν πάντα ποιεῖς ἵνα σε ἀποκτείνω, ἐγὼ δὲ κύνα ὑλακτοῦντα οὐ φονεύω (Suet. *Vesp.* 13.)

[18] It is sufficiently clear that Petronius was the adherent of no particular philosophy. Some of the toughness of his attitude to life may be a native Roman or Italian attitude rather than hellenised philosophy: this seems to have been true of Tacitus, who embraced what was almost a caricature of "Roman-ness" and despised philosophy (Syme 553). D. R. Dudley has argued in the case of Blossius of Cumae, (*Journal of Roman Studies* XXXI, 1941, 94–99), that certain native characteristics could appear to be the traits of a radical Greek philosophical posture, when in fact they were nothing of the kind. Blossius (and the elder Cato) suggest automatically one kind of philosophy; Petronius another, and it has

him down to any particular position. The *Satyricon* itself has many times been regarded as enshrining a debased Epicurean way of life, but much of it could just as easily be taken as a Cynic or Stoic tract. Apart from the attested Stoic/Cynic interest in and influence upon the imaginative novel in antiquity,[19] and the Cynic roots of the Menippean satire which informs much of the *Satyricon*, there is in the tone of the work something reminiscent of the ἀπάθεια, ἀναιδεία,, αὐτάρκεια, παρρησία, and especially σπουδογέλοιον of the Cynics.[20] The behaviour of the characters is different from that of the mildly hedonic Epicureans; it is more like the immediate, pleasureless fulfilment of lusts that was

long been fashionable to regard Petronius as an Epicurean both on account of the tone of his works and in particular because fg. 27 *"Primus in orbe deos fecit timor"* recalls Epicurean themes. This aspect of Petronius has impressed writers as diverse as W. E. H. Lecky, *A History of European Morals* ed. 3, Vol, I 162, London 1913, and G. Highet, Petronius the Moralist, *Transactions of the American Philological Association*, 1941, 176–194. The most systematic interpretation along these lines is that of Oscar Raith, *Petronius ein Epicureer*, Diss. Erlangen 1963. There are, however, elements not only in Petronius' novel, but in his life as Tacitus narrates it which are susceptible of a Cynic interpretation. These elements were probably given their particular flavour by "Fannius," if as it is reasonable to suppose, he was the source of Tacitus' account of Petronius' life. Petronius' *neglegentia* can be given the colour either of Epicurean ἀταραξία or Cynic ἀναιδεία. The attitude to pleasure which we can impute to Petronius on the basis of Tacitus' account or from the novel is sufficiently complex to bear at once the Epicurean and Cynic interpretations. There is also an undeniable element of σπουδογέλοιον (Highet) which is more emphatic than would merely be the case if it was nothing but an inheritance from the Menippean literary tradition. There is in fact much common ground between these otherwise antipathetic Hellenistic philosophies. (Diog. Laertius IX 119, 8, presents Epicurus' own attack on the Cynics). Raith, 53, admits Cynic connections in Petronius, but seeks to dissolve away their importance by emphasising that Petronius was an aristocrat (which is not strictly the case) and so by definition anti-Cynic. But we must recall that Thrasea Paetus and other prominent members of the "opposition" were under Cynic influence – Thrasea was certainly no less "aristocratic" than Petronius. See also R. Hirzel, *Der Dialog*, Lips. 1895, II, 38, for a discussion of the Cynic as well as the Epicurean traces in Petronius' work. Hirzel adduces parallels for the coexistence of Cynic and Epicurean influences in the same author, who may not be completely aware of the conflict between them. Further, the Cynics seem to have accepted a materialist interpretation of the natural world: E. Zeller *Die Philosophie der Griechen in ihrer geschichtlichen Entwicklung* 2, 1. 289–9.

[19] Hirzel, *ibid.;* For resemblances between Petronius' novel and Menippean satire, E. Rohde, *Der Griechische Roman*, Lips. 1914, 265–269; on Cynic polities and their relation to the Greek novel: 251–260. See also Rohde's discussion: "Zum Griechischen Roman," *Rheinisches Museum für Philologie*, 48, 1893, 110–139.

[20] Dudley, *A History of Cynicism*, London 1937, 41, 95; Highet, *op. cit.* 188. For the parodic element in Petronius' work: E. Courtney, "Parody and Literary Allusion in Menippean Satire", *Philologus*, Bd. 106, Heft 1/2, 1962, 86–100.

expounded by the older members of the Cynic school.[21] Also, in the characters of the *Satyricon* we have Cynic beggary, and a carelessness of life which (*pace* Highet) could be thought of as Cynic rather than Epicurean.[22] Of course the characters of the novel are (with one or two exceptions) profoundly unhappy people, and this might suggest that

---

[21] The official Cynic attitude to pleasure is disapproval, and ἀπάθεια represents resistance both to pleasure and to pain (*cf.*, ἀταραξία but this was not necessarily reflected in the practices of individual Cynics (Lucian Vit. Auct. 10; Dio Chrysostom 8, 20: Lucian, *Runaways* 19.) There is a fair consensus of authorities that early Cynic writings, especially of the utopist political category, were characterised by suggestions of promiscuity and incest (Diog. L. VI 72). Dudley, *Hist. Cyn.* 26, 36. F. Sayre, *Diogenes of Sinope, A Study of Greek Cynicism*, Baltimore 1938, 4, 5, 25. R. Hoïstad, *Cynic Hero and Cynic King*, Uppsala 1948, 146, 178. *Cf.* K. von Fritz, "Quellen-Untersuchungen zu Leben und Philosophie des Diogenes von Sinope," *Philologus*, Suppl. XVIII, Hft. II, 55–56, where he interprets the Philodemus tradition (see Zeller II 1, 284) which denies the existence of a Diogenes-polity, as being based upon an attempt of later Stoics to "bowdlerise" their philosophical ancestors, the Cynics.

[22] See notes 18 and 21 above. It is not clear that Epicureans as well as Cynic philosophers positively accepted suicide as being a possible means of dealing with a hostile environment; although Highet's suggestion that Petronius' suicide was an Epicurean one (rather than any other kind) is plausible, its basis rests merely on the distinction drawn by Tacitus between Petronius' and Seneca's suicides, and this distinction was thrown in to deliberate relief by Tacitus for his own anti-philosophical purposes (*cf.* Syme 553). In fact there was not an "Epicurean Suicide" in the sense, that there was a "Cynic or Stoic Suicide". Nothing like an εὔλογος ἐξαγωγή established itself in Epicurean thought, though according to Cicero, Epicurus mentioned suicide, and suggested that one could depart from life *tanquam e theatro* if it became unbearable (Cicero *Fin.* 1, 15, 44). See also Lucr. III 944, which suggests a gentle removal from life if it becomes too wearisome. (*Cf.* Seneca ch. XXVI, *de vita beata* 19). Lucretius is said by Jerome to have committed suicide, but even if this was so, it must be recalled that he was not a typical Epicurean. W. E. H. Lecky, *op. cit.* 215, mentions several Epicurean suicides. Also, Karl August Geiger, *Der Selbstmord im Klassischen Altertum, Historisch-kritische Abhandlung*, Augsburg 1888, 14. It looks as if the Cynics/Stoics regarded suicide as an important philosphical act, but the Epicureans simply acknowledged its possibility in cases of extreme distress, – an attitude which is common to many of the legal codes of ancient cities, which permitted the old and infirm to withdraw themselves from life when it became too painful: Geiger, 59–63; *R.–E.* "Selbstmord" (Thalheim) 1135. It is possible (with Highet) to see this kind of "voluntary" withdrawal in Petronius' suicide, but it is not necessary to agree that it is specifically Epicurean, though the notion *tanquam e theatro* seems to fit in well with Petronius' attitude to life. However, it is not less plausible to suppose that Petronius' "suicide" was not so much a withdrawal from a theatre as a theatrical act itself, an act of black comedy. It is a deliberate parody of the Stoic suicide, with all the details of the latter presented with considered Galgenhumor. Also it is noteworthy that the suicides mentioned in the text of Petronius are not of the quietist kind, but are violent and egotistic, chapters 94, 101, 107, 108: – they were also pretences!

an Epicurean author was, after the fashion of his school,[23] satirising and attacking the Cynics. If this is the case, the author is certainly possessed of sufficient knowledge of the Cynicising "beatniks" of his time to empathise with them in his delineation of their characters.

Although it is impossible for us to determine with certainty the philosophical position of the author, there is however much material even in the surviving portion of the novel[24] for a Cynicising or Stoicising interpreter to convert to his own use. Unless the lost part of the novel is very different in its emphasis, it is quite probable that "Fannius" would be encouraged further by the flavour of the novel to put a Cynicising gloss on the events of the novelist's life. We can see this kind of interpretation casting its shadow in the account of Petronius' life in the *Annales*.[25] In the novelist's carelessness of himself and his outspokenness, we have factors which fit into the picture of ἀναιδεία and παρρησία that characterised the Cynic Sage. We may recall the ostentatious and even arrogant self-contempt of Crates taking his son to the brothel and pointing out that here his father was married,[26] as well as numerous anecdotes about the Cynics which, like Petronius'

[23] Epicurus himself is said to have regarded the Cynics as enemies of the Greek way of life (Diog. L. 9. 119) *cf.* Crönert, *Kolotes und Menedemos* 36; Dudley 106.

[24] The *Trau* MS. has the subscription: *Petronii Arbitri Satyri fragmenta expliciunt ex libro quinto decimo et sexto decimo:* but at least one fragment attributed to Petronius may come from Book XIV. See the discussions of Buecheler, (Heraeus) *Petronii Saturae,* Berlin 1922, vi. vi. and Konrad Müller, *Petronii Arbitri Satiricon,* München 1961, xxix–xxxi.

[25] It was not difficult to inject a flavour of Cynicism or Stoicism in such cases, given the many precedents of abusing the emperor provided by non-philosophers. Vestinus, the consul, a close friend of Nero, engaged in abusive jests at his expense and incurred his enmity: *ceterum Neroni odium adversus Vestinum ex intima sodalitate coeperat, dum hic ignaviam principis penitus cognitam despicit, ille ferociam amici metuit, saepe asperis facetiis inlusus, quae ubi multum ex vero traxere, acrem sui memoriam relinquunt (Annales 15, 68, 4).* At *Annales* I 12, 6, *ferocia* is used of the outspokenness of Asinius Pollio, and Furneaux notes (*ad loc.*) that Dio uses παρρησία to characterise this bitterness of speech. The use of this Cynicising word illustrates the impression of philosophical posture which would be given by certain types of Roman (irrespective of the actual philosophical affiliations of the person who gives the impression). Antistius' *probra in Neronem composita* brought about his death (*Ann.* 16, 21, 2). Lucan is said to have been responsible for a *famosum carmen* against Nero and his friends (*C. Suetonii Tranquilli quae supersunt omnia* ed. Roth Lips. 1882, 229–300). H. Musurillo compares the writings of Fannius and Helvidius with the "protocol" literature of Alexandria which contained attacks upon the emperors (*Acts of the Pagan Martyrs,* Oxford 1954, 241).

[26] Diog. L. 7, 87–88: Crates regarded human institutions as contemptible. For the satirical nature of the Cynic utopia, see H. C. Baldry's comments on Crates' Πήρα: "Zeno's Ideal State," *Journal of Hellenic Studies* 1959, 3–15: 14 especially.

neglegentia sui, aim at an impression of *simplicity*. Also, apart from the
novel, the final outburst in which he describes in detail Nero's vices
has parallels in the scurrilous attacks made upon Nero by Vestinus
and Antistius; it also is paralleled in its abusiveness by the foul-mouthed
writings attributed to such respectable fathers of the Stoic school as
Chrysippus,[27] and by the attacks upon emperors recorded in the "protocol" literature of Alexandria.[28] These factors provide possible material
for a writer, who favoured the "Stoic Opposition", to over-interpret or
over-emphasise in his writings. We do not know whether the writer of
the life of Petronius which was Tacitus' source, and whom we not im-
probably regard as Fannius, had first-hand knowledge of Petronius'
account of Nero's vices, or not.[29] Nor do we know whether Tacitus
had read it independently. Many of the works of the genre[30] were destroyed. In the case of some more publishable books than this personal
outburst, we hear that one copy was preserved.[31] It is not likely,
though it is always possible, that a copy, or at least rough notes,
survived of an attack which must surely have been dictated to
somebody in the first instance, though Petronius' providence in the
case of his signet might suggest that he would order the notes to be
destroyed. It is more likely that some notion of the contents of this
attack was preserved by oral tradition which stemmed from the
reminiscences of the person to whom the work was dictated.

"Fannius" may have embodied some of this tradition, and Tacitus
himself may have been aware of it in his "life" of Petronius. Neither
Fannius nor Tacitus need have seen a copy. We can hardly deny the
possibility that the source account (and/or Tacitus' account of Petronius)
was coloured not so much by this oral tradition as by the novel itself.

Fannius' interpretation of Petronius' life may have been given extra
encouragement by the known fact that Petronius was accused of being
on friendly terms with a leader of the philosophical opposition. It is
not likely that Tigellinus would have accused Petronius of this friendship if Petronius had been completely beyond suspicion. The cunning
of a man like Tigellinus might well have led him to suggest the plausible

---

[27] Diog. L. 7, 188 mentions the notorious foulness of Chrysippus' language
even when he was writing about serious technical matters.
[28] Musurillo, *op. cit.*
[29] Nevertheless Tacitus (and possibly his source) seems to have a precise
enough notion of its scope and contents.
[30] Tac. *Agricola* 2; Marx, *op. cit.* 87.
[31] Pliny, *Epist.* 7, 19, 5; Marx, 87–88.

as being easier to persuade even upon Nero, than the impossible. Though, again, we must remember the hysteria both of the emperor and of the public at large at this time. We cannot be certain. Nor can we be sure how many of the facts of Petronius' life "Fannius" could know in isolation from the philosophical matrix in which both the time of his death and his fellowship in "martyrdom" with distinguished philosophers embedded them. Fannius' own sources of information were probably irremediably distorted by family predilection, which saw the victims as forming more of a cohesive group than was in fact the case.

Tacitus is interested in the contrast of Petronius' death with that of Seneca.[32] He has already contrasted Seneca's death with the tough soldierly death of Subrius Flavus the tribune, which he evidently regards as a healthy antidote to Seneca's premortuary lecture with friends taking notes: *ipsa rettuli verba, quia non, ut Senecae, vulgata erant, nec minus nosci decebat militaris viri sensus incomptos et validos* (*Ann.* XV, 67). In the tribune's last grim jest about the inadequacy of the grave dug for him: *ne hoc quidem ex disciplina*, Tacitus probably saw the distinctly Roman, unphilosophical toughness that was an enduring and reassuring characteristic even in the worst of times. In Petronius also, he sees an intellectual who can die without the consolations of philosophical flummery. In propounding an account of Petronius which implies that he might in fact be innocent of personal complicity in the worst of Nero's vicious lucubrations, Tacitus asserts on his own behalf as well as that of Petronius the detached and intact nature of the artist and historian. He could scarcely fail to recall that he agreed with much of Petronius' attitude to oratory,[33] and that he himself had written accounts of human viciousness without deserving to be accounted depraved himself.

---

[32] For Tacitus' fanatical and anti-philosophical "Roman-ness," Syme 553. Tacitus would ignore any philosophical gloss given to Petronius' life and death by any such source as Fannius; he interprets the apparently parodic nature of Petronius' death as a deliberate piece of anti-philosophical satire, and does not seem to see any Cynicism or Epicureanism in it. *Cf.* note 25, and D. R. Dudley's interpretation of the life of Blossius (T. Gracchus' associate) as being Campanian in his attitude rather than philosophical. Note 18 above.

[33] E. Paratore, *Il Satyricon di Petronio* II, ch. 1, 19, Firenze 1933; Tacito 1954, 206–8.

"EATING PEOPLE IS RIGHT": PETRONIUS 141
AND A ΤΟΠΟΣ

Eumolpus, desperately striving to fend off Crotoniate *captatores*, stipulates that whoever wishes to benefit under the terms of his will must publicly eat flesh of his dead body. K. Müller notes an allusion here to Herodotus, 3. 99;[1] O. Raith calls the whole suggestion of 141: *eine Kynische Posse*.[2] A well established τόπος seems to fill up the void between these two points of reference. In this brief discussion I propose to comment on this passage of Petronius in the light of the topic of ἀνδροβορία or ἀνδροφαγία. To facilitate discussion, I shall refer to different sections of the relevant part of 141 as (a) (b) (c) (d) in the following manner:

(a) 141, 2: *"omnes qui in testamento meo legata habent praeter libertos meos hac condicione percipient quae dedi, si corpus meum in partes conciderint et astante populo comederint"*

There is a break in the continuity of the text after this passage, whose words, framed in legalistic style, support Raith's view up to a point. We may recall such passages from the Cynic πολιτεῖαι as the following: τί σοί ἔδοξε τὰ Ζήνωνος ἤ τὰ Διογένους καὶ Κλεάνθους, ὁπόσα περιέχουσιν αἱ βίβλοι αὐτῶν διδάσκουσαι· ἀνθρωποβορίας, πατέρας μέν ὑπὸ ἰδίων τέκνων ἔψεσθαι καὶ βιβρώσκεσθαι καὶ, εἴ τις οὐ βούλοιτο ἤ μέρος τι τῆς μυσαρᾶς τροφῆς ἀπορρίψειεν, αὐτὸν κατεσθίεσθαι τὸν μὴ φαγόντα: Theophilus ad Autol. III 5 p 119c: Von Arnim, *Stoicorum Veterum Fragmenta*, fg. 584. *cf. ibid.* Vol. I fg. 254. Vol. III fg. 746: Chrysippus advocates ἀνθρωποβορεῖν in a context which permits incest and the like; 747: Diog. L. VII, 188: VII, 121: γεύσασθαι τε καὶ ἀνθρωπίνων σαρκῶν κατὰ περίστασιν; 748, 749, 750 *etc.* Note that in the Petronius passage

---

[1] K. Müller, *Petronii Arbitri Satyricon*, München, 1961, apparat. crit. on ch. 141.
[2] *Petronius, Ein Epicureer*, Diss. Erlangen, 1963, 52.

and in fg 584 there is a mandate to the effect that the cannibalism shall be under some kind of public scrutiny, *astante populo*.[3] If a tabu is to be broken, there must be proof that it has been broken, and this necessitates some form of witness. It is possible that this idea in Petronius comes directly from Cynic πολιτεῖαι which (like Cynic tragedies)[4] are sufficiently extravagant and paradoxical to provide interesting raw material for an author whose "day was night". They are deliberate attempts to reverse usually accepted νόμοι.[5] If, however, with Raith, we regard whatever philosophical influences there were in Petronius as being more Epicurean than Cynic,[6] we might envisage the possibility that Petronius learned about the extraordinary contents of the πολιτεῖαι from such Epicurean writers as Philodemus.[7] The lack of precise differentiation between Cynic and Stoic notions of the earlier period might have been used by Petronius (if we run the thesis that he was at least "pro-Epicurean") to discredit Seneca's Stoicism, though this seems less likely than the view put forward by J. P. Sullivan, that Seneca's literary theory and practice were important targets for an author who was, on the evidence, more artist than philosopher.[8]

   (b) 141, 3–4: *"apud quasdam gentes scimus adhuc legem servari,*
         ut a propinquis suis consumantur defuncti, adeo
         quidem ut obiurgentur aegri frequenter, quod carnem
         suam faciant peiorem. his admoneo amicos meos ne
         recusent quae iubeo, sed quibus animis devoverint
         spiritum meum, eisdem etiam corpus consumant."

A break in the continuity of the text follows: then

   141, 5: *"excaecabat pecuniae ingens fama oculos animosque*
      miserorum.

      Gorgias paratus erat exsequi"

[3] 141, 2. *cf.* the passage quoted (Von Arnim fg. 584), the mandate implied by εἴ τις οὐ βούλοιτο κτλ, in contrast with κατὰ περίστασιν Diog. L, VII, 121, also, VI, 73, of Diogenes the Cynic, which is related at least in spirit to the Petronius passage: μηδ' ἀνόσιον εἶναι τὸ καὶ τῶν ἀνθρωπείων κρεῶν ἅψασθαι, ὡς δῆλον ἐκ τῶν ἀλλοτρίων ἐθῶν κτλ (quoted by Raith, 69).

[4] Diog. L, VI. 80; Dümmler, *Antisthenica* 12; Diogenes of Sinope, *R.–E.* (Natorp) 769; K. von Fritz, "Quellen–Untersuchungen zu Leben und Philosophie des Diogenes von Sinope," *Philologus Suppl.* XVIII, Hft. II, 88; D. R. Dudley, *A History of Cynicism*, London, 1937, 25–27, 30; A.–H. Chroust, *Socrates, Man and Myth*, London, 1957, 161.

[5] παραχαράττειν τὸ νόμισμα: Dudley 31.

[6] Raith's view: but see Kaimowitz's review, *A. J. P.*, Vol. 87, no. 348, 478–81.

[7] Crönert, *Kolotes und Menedemos* 63, 53 ff. on ἀνθρωποφαγία.

[8] J. P. Sullivan, *The Satyricon of Petronius, A Literary Study*, London, 1968, 193 ff.

"Gorgias," presumably a *captator*, has a good sophist name: he is prepared to comply with Eumolpus' stipulation. There is no necessity to suppose that Petronius was directly acquainted with any of the passages of Herodotus that deal with anthropophagy, or in particular, Hdt 3, 99.[9] Petronius' reading of the classics seems to have been quite wide, though we must differentiate between works that he knew at first (or decent second) hand and work that he mentioned.[10] It is impossible to say for certain whether or not he really knew the works of Thucydides, whom he mentions once,[11] though he might well have had some acquaintance with an author who was so popular in imperial times. Even if he knew Thucydides, we need not infer that he had any knowledge of Herodotus: his reference to the practices *apud quasdam gentes* need in fact only come from rhetorical schools.

The theme of cannibalism is an old one. Eating human flesh was tabu in the ancient world. Kronos was not highly regarded for devouring his children. The Thyestes story was the germ of generations of tragedy. Achilles is in a paroxysm of anger when he says that he could eat Hector raw (*Iliad* 22, 346 ff), but in fact he does not. The man-eating Cyclops in the *Odyssey* is, in point of civilisation, the lowest of the low. Abstention from human flesh, in the Archaic Greek view,, is connected with the possession of νόμοι. On this question, F. Heinimann, in his *Nomos und Physis* 61–2[12] quotes Hesiod's contrast between mankind, which has νόμος and δίκαι, and does not eat fellow human beings, and the rest of animal creation, which does eat fellow creatures.[13] Heinimann points out that Homer's Cyclops, a man-devourer: οὔτε δίκας εὖ εἰδότα οὔτε θέμιστας[14], nor have the ἀνδροφάγοι mentioned by Herodotus, 4, 106:[15] ἀνδροφάγοι δέ ἀγριότατα πάντων ἀνθρώπων ἔχουσι ἤθεα οὔτε δίκην νομίζοντες οὔτε νόμῳ οὐδενὶ χρεώμενοι (*cf.* 4. 105).

This theory of anthropophagy is not accepted so uncritically in the

---

[9] *Hdt*, III, 38, IV, 26, 105, 106. *cf.* I, 216 and *R.–E.* (Tomaschek) *s.v.* Androboria.

[10] A. Rini, *Petronius in Italy*, N. Y. 159. *cf.* the list of classic writers quoted in *Satyricon*, chs. 1–2. Whether or not he knew such writers as Hipponax at first hand is debatable: Latte, *Hermes* 64, 1929, 384 ff; O. Masson, *Les Fragments du Poète Hipponax*, Paris 1962, 150.

[11] 2, 8.

[12] Basel 1945.

[13] 276 ff: part of a piece of advice to Perses: it follows quite naturally the "beast-fable" of lines 202–211; see F. A. Paley's notes *ad loc The Epics of Hesiod*, London 1861.

[14] *Odyssey*, 9, 215.

[15] Heinimann, 62, thinks that Herodotus has *Odyssey* 9, 215 in mind. *cf.* Tacitus' description of the Fenni as a Naturvolk: *Germania* 46.

period of the Fifth Century "Aufklärung," but the most clear example
of the "relativistic" approach to the question – Herodotus' account of
Darius' confrontation of the Greeks with the Kallatiai, – depends
quite probably upon traditional Ionian sceptical relativism (of the
kind that is exampled in Xenophanes) as much as upon the beginnings
of sophistic criticism.[16] The passage, like that which is principally our
concern in Petronius, and like those quoted in the Cynic-Stoic tradition, treats of burial: the Greeks burn the bodies of their deceased
parents; the Kallatiai eat theirs. Both sides are profoundly shocked
at the practices of the other.[17] The lesson emerges from the comparison
that even if people are given a selection of νόμοι to choose from, they
will not by any means inevitably opt for the best, but will adhere to
their own, as being the best. Heinimann, p. 81, regards this as a Sophist-
influenced view: certainly it has much in common with the relativist
views of the third quarter of the Fifth Century B. C.: it is in fact a
commonplace, as is illustrated by its occurrence in ΔΙΣΣΟΙ ΛΟΓΟΙ 2,
18, 26.[18] Like other commonplaces, for instance: that of the comparison
between the customs of animals and man, this one passed over to post
sophistic philosophers, in this case, the writers of Cynic-Stoic πολιτεῖαι.[19]

(c) 141, 6–8:   *"de stomachi tui recusatione non habeo quod*
timeam. sequetur imperium, si promiseris illi pro
unius horae fastidio multorum bonorum pensatio-
nem. operi modo oculos et finge te non humana
viscera sed centies sestertium comesse. accedit huc
quod aliqua inveniemus blandimenta, quibus saporem
mutemus. neque enim ulla caro per se placet, sed
arte quadam corrumpitur et stomacho conciliatur
averso."

A sophistry, conflating human and non-human in a relativistic fashion
reminiscent of (b): possibly a commonplace which was employed in
the arguments of the schools' themes cf. Petronius *Satyricon* ch. 1).
These words may have Cynic antecedents as well, but there is no evidence to hand. Sophistic and other philosophical comparisons between

---

[16] Heinimann 80–1. Xenophanes Fg. 15, H. Diels, *Poetarum Philosophorum
Fragmenta*, Berlin, 1901, 40.

[17] *Dissoi Logoi* 2. 14.

[18] Hdt 3, 36: Gomperz, *Sophistik und Rhetorik* Berlin, 1912, 164.

[19] Heinimann 146–7; R. Hirzel, *Themis Dike und Verwandtes*,Lips. 1907,
212–220; Sinclair, *C. R.* 1948, 61–2; Rankin, *Hermes* 93. 4. 1965, 417–8; cf. Mayor,
C. R. 1898, 93–6.

man and other animals have roots not only in the early beast-fable,
but in proverbs, and indeed in even more primitive ways of regarding
non-human species which can conveniently be drawn together under
the name "totemism."[20] Running parallel to the sophistry of people
like Eumolpus, we find such examples of folk-thinking[21] (as against
philosophical relativism) in the equation of man and beast which
Habinnas' remarks imply 66. 6: *ego contra plus libram (ursinae) comedi,
nam ipsum aprum sapiebat. et si, inquam, ursus homuncionem comest,
quanto magis homencio debet ursum comesse?* And another aspect
of man's relation to animals is contained in the story of the *Versipellis*
(62).[22] The very Roman phrase: *sestertium centies commesse*[23] suggests
that equation of food, death and decay, which has recently been made
the basis of an interpretation of the *Satyricon:*[24] a related theme is to
be seen in the proverbial locution: *paratus fuit quadrantem mordicus
de stercore tollere* (43. 1).

(d) 141, 9–11: *"quod si exemplis quoque vis probari consilium,
Saguntini oppressi ab Hannibale humanas edere
carnes, nec hereditatem expectabant. Petelini idem
fecerunt in ultima fame, nec quicquam aliud in hac
epulatione captabant nisi tantum ne esurirent. cum
esset Numantia a Scipione capta, inventae sunt matres
quae liberorum suorum tenerent semesa in sinu corpora."*

Particularly persuasive to Romans as a justification for anthropophagy
would be stress of siege. Explanations of this kind would involve
such historical examples[25] as those mentioned here, which were familiar
enough to educated Romans.[26] It is not hard to envisage a school theme
which calls upon the student in rhetoric to defend anthropophagy:
such an exercise would not be any more extreme than some of those

---

[20] Freud, *Totem and Taboo*, Std. Ed. transl. Strachey, Vol. XIII.
[21] Rankin, *op. cit.* 417.
[22] J. G. Frazer, *Golden Bough*, vol. I. 310–320.
[23] Martial V, 71 – an often quoted occurrance of this metaphor.
[24] W. Arrowsmith, "Luxury and Death in the *Satyricon*," *Arion*, Vol. V. no.
3, Autumn 1966, 304–331.
[25] S. F. Bonner, *Roman Declamation*, California 1949, 62.
[26] See the collected references *ad loc* in the commentaries of J. A. Wouweren
Amsterdam 1626, Hadrianides, Amsterdam 1669, Burmann, Utrecht 1709
(also Gonsalius de Salas' notes printed in Vol II of this work). Most critics now
opt for Petelia (with Müller). See further W. Arrowsmith, *Petronius the Satyricon*,
Ann Arbor 1959, (note, to transl. of 141); J. P. Sullivan, *Petronius the Satyricon
and Fragments*, Penguin, 1965, 204 (note to translation of 141).

which are cited in 1, 1–3. The whole presentation of the theme in the present passage is obviously rhetorical, after the fashion of such an exercise.

To conclude, if we join threads (a) (b) (c) (d) together, we envisage a τόπος which ranges from Herodotean-sophistic points of view (influences no doubt by early "Ionian" sources as well) to the school θέσεις of First Century A. D., Rome. A quite direct reference to Cynic πολιτεία may well be present also, together with a flavour of the folk ideation which characterises parts of the *Satyricon*. In short, this passage has, culturally speaking, some historical depth. It would be interesting to know how many of the strands of reference Petronius was aware of, though whether or not he had conscious, detailed, knowledge makes little difference to our appreciation of the density of texture which, consummate artist as he was, he achieved in this and other parts of his surviving work.

DID TACITUS QUOTE PETRONIUS?

nam illi dies per somnum, nox officiis et oblectamentis vitae
transigebatur; utque alios industria, ita hunc ignavia ad famam
protulerat, habebaturque non ganeo et profligator, ut plerique sua
haurentium, sed erudito luxu. ac dicta factaque eius quanto solu-
tiora et quandam sui neglegentiam praeferentia, tanto gratius in
speciem simplicitatis accipiebantur.

H. Bogner's discussion, "Petronius bei Tacitus" (*Hermes* 76, 1941,
223-4) contains the suggestion that Tacitus' use of the word
simplicitas in the characterisation of Petronius (*Annales*, 16, 18) may
mean that Tacitus himself and in person saw the word in its original
context of the poem of *Satyricon* ch. 132: 15: *quid me constricta*
spectatis fronte Catones/damnatisque novae simplicitatis opus? I would
like to argue in support of Bogner's view, and though I would not wish
to commit myself strictly on the "programmatic" function of *sim-*
plicitas in the *Satyricon*, I would not deny that this function, which
was enunciated by Stubbe,[1] and largely accepted by Bogner,[2] must be
admitted to some extent. It is important for the argument of connection between Petronius' poem and Tacitus' text that the word *simpli-*
citas in the poem should itself be somehow notable. Whether or not we

---

[1] Heinz Stubbe, "Die Verseinlagen im Petron", *Philologus*, Supplementband
XXV, Heft 2, Leipzig 1933: iv. *Das Programm des Autors*, 150-153. S. regards
simplicitas as: "Der unschuldige, unverbildete, nicht heuchelnde Realismus des
Werkes (*opus* auch = Gattung, Quintil. *Inst.*, X, 1, 67 und 69) dem Inhalt so-
wohl wie der Sprache nach."

[2] *Op. cit.*, 224: "Es ist anzunehmen, dass die angeführten Verse des Petronius gleich zu seiner zeit, beim Erscheinen des Werkes als programmatisch auf-
gefasst werden. Dann hegt der Schluss nahe, dass Tacitus sie (wie überhaupt den
Roman des Petronius) kannte und für die Charakteristik des Mannes auch dessen
eigene Worte benutzte, in denen Petronius für seine gewagten Schilderungen
die *simplicitas* in Anspruch nimmt."

accept Bickel's[3] emphasis upon the fashionable use of *simplicitas* in the Silver Age (a point which he urges against the "programmatic" hypothesis, but which could as easily be used to support it by its implication that the word *simplicitas* might catch a reader's attention), the common enough occurrence of the word in Tacitus[4] to indicate personal traits renders prima facie unlikely a verbal connection between the poem and the passage in the *Annales* which depends upon the word alone.

However, if we look at the phrases in Tacitus and Petronius in which the word *simplicitas* is embedded, we may see, I suggest, both of them in an oxymoron, which, though it is of the kind to which *simplex, simplicitas* etc. especially lend themselves (viz. *simplex munditiis*, Hor. *Odes* I, 5, 5), nevertheless may well indicate a connection between the two texts which is more than coincidental. For the two phrases, *nova simplicitas* and *in speciem simplicitatis* seem to convey the same meaning, which is of a "simplicity" that is not "simple" at all. In the poem, the adjective *novus* gives the lie to any notion of genuine simplicity, and the imagined "Catones" may be supposed to object not so much to *simplicitas* in itself (even if *simplicitas* by itself be translated in an unlikely way as "naturalism," the Catones would not in their Old Roman or Stoic character disapprove.) Their objections would naturally be directed to something which purported to be one thing and was in fact another, in short, to its falsity, – or else perhaps to its mere newness. The semantic field of *novus* is wide, and includes meanings such as "weird," "outrageous". Petronius probably used the word in full awareness of its ambiguity, and of the "Catonian" dislike both of novelty and a lack of genuineness. If we suppose Tacitus as a reader of the *Satyricon*, his own use of *novus*[5] etc. can be adduced to support the view that he would have regarded Petronius' *novae*

---

[3] E. Bickel, Petrons *simplicitas* bei Tacitus, Rheinisches Museum, 99, 1941, 269–271.

[4] As a personal characteristic: *Histories* 3, 86, 7; 4, 86, 9; *Annales* VI, 5, 13, and of Petronius: 16, 5, 13.

[5] For example, a plain case of *novus* with the meaning "outrageous" etc. *Annales* XIV 2, 14, *seu credibilior novae libidinis meditatio in ea visa est quae puellaribus annis* etc.– of Agrippina's possible intention of incest with Nero *cf. novitas* note 6 *infra*; an ambiguous use is to be seen in Tacitus' phrase which, at *Annales*, XI, 25, 19, he attributes to the consul speaking of Claudius: *nova in rem publicam merita non usitatis vocabulis honoranda*. The historian here puts ambiguity into the mouth of a historical personage who might possibly have employed it, if he felt it might not be perceived, but the ambiguity is entirely of Tacitus' creation, and no report of the actual words is suggested.

simplicitatis as an ambiguous use of *novus*. A pointed example, involving a related form, occurs in the very passage which discusses Nero's vices and the account of them written by Petronius before he died: *novitas*[6] is used to characterise their outrageousness and perversity (*Annales*, 16, 19, 5). Tacitus' own phrase *in speciem simplicitatis* might on this interpretation be a paraphrase of *nova simplicitas*, in that it gives the lie to the notion that Petronius was at all "simple." The point about *simplicitas, simplex* etc. is that they should not mean anything "weird" or "strange".[7]

All that I have tried to do is to reinforce the hypothesis of verbal reminiscence. Even if I am right in doing so, the verbal reminiscence in itself does not entail rigidly that Tacitus must have read the *Satyricon* "at first hand." He may have heard the phrase quoted orally or read it in some intermediary author of *exitus*-biographies,[8] for it is reasonable to suppose that very few copies of the *Satyricon* long survived their author.

---

[6] *Sed flagitia principis sub nominibus exoletorum feminarumque et novitate cuiusque stupri perscripsit, atque obsignata misit Neroni; Annales* XVI, 18, 7. and II, 24, 2, *quanto violentior cetero mari Oceanus et truculentia caeli praestat Germania, tantum illa clades novitate et magnitudine excessit, hostilibus circum litoribus, aut ita vasto et profundo ut credatur novissimum mare. Cf. Hist.*, I, 75, 6: *novitate vultus – prodebantur; Annales*, XVI,   30, 5, *Druide novitate aspectus – perculere militem.*

[7] Much less, anything lacking in candour or involving complicated vice; *cf.* Ovid, *Metamorphoses*, 15, 20–1. *Quid meruere boves, animal sine fraude dolisque/ innocuum simplex?* For a modern version of simplicity that is not simple, see F. Fitzgeralds' *Tender is the Night*, Bodley Head edit. Vol. II, p. 91: the description of the behaviour of Dr. and Mrs. Diver, and the ingénue Rosemary's misapprehension of it as simplicity. Fitzgerald was strongly influenced by Petronius; see Paul L. MacKendrick, "The Great Gatsby and Trimalchio," *Classical Journal*, Vol. 45, No. 7, 1950, pp. 307–314.

[8] F. A. Marx, "Tacitus und die Literatur der exitus illustrium virorum," *Philologus*, XCII, N. F. XLVI, 1937, 83–103.

SHORT BIBLIOGRAPHY

Note: Abbreviations: Apart from the usual abbreviations of the titles of well-known works and periodicals (*e.g.* *R-E* for *Real-Encyclopaedie*, *PLM* for *Poetae Latini Minores, etc.*) I have sometimes used abbreviations in the notes which are not familiar but which I hope are easily understandable from the context, *e.g.* "*R.R.*" near "Syme" will stand for "Roman Revolution", or *D.P.* in the context with "H. Herter" will be "De Priapo".

TEXTS, COMMENTARIES, AND TRANSLATIONS

Petronius, The Satyricon, translated by William Arrowsmith, New York, 1960
Petronii Satirae et Liber Priapeorum, ed. F. Buecheler, Berlin 1871
Titi Petronii Arbitri Satyricôn quae supersunt cum integris notis Doctorum Virorum Commentariis; et Notes Nicolai Heinsii et Guilielmi Goesii nunc primum editis, accedunt Jani Dousae Praecidanea, D. Jos Ant Gonsali de Salas Commenta, variae Dissertationes et Praefationes, etc., curante Petro Burmanno, Trajecti ad Rhenum 1709
Petronii Saturae recensuit Franciscus Buecheler *exemplar ex editione anni MDCCCLXII anastatice iteratum; adiectae sunt Varronis et Senecae Saturae similesque reliquiae ex editione sexta anni MDCCCCXII* a Guilielmo Heraeo *curata repetita et supplementa*, Berlin, 1958
Pétrone, Le Satyricon, Texte établi et traduit par A. Ernout, Paris 1967
Petronii Cena Trimalchionis, mit Deutscher übersetzung und erklärenden Anmerkungen, von Ludwig Friedländer, Leipzig 1891
Titi Petronii Arbitri Equitis Romani Satyricon, cum Fragmento nuper Tragurii reperto; Accedunt diversorum Poetarum Lusus in Priapum, Pervigilium Veneris, Ausonii cento nuptialis, Cupido crucifixus, Epistolae de Cleopatra et alia nonnulla, omnia commentariis et notis Doctorum Virorum illustrata, concinnante Michaele Hadrianide, Amstelodami 1669
Petronius, with an English Translation by Michael Heseltine; *Seneca, Apocolocyntosis*, with an English Translation by W. H. D. Rouse, (Loeb Classical Series) London 1916
Petronii Cena Trimalchionis, edited with critical and explanatory notes and translated into English Prose, W. D. Lowe, Cambridge, 1905
Petronius, The Satyricon, translated by J. M. Mitchell, with an Introduction and notes, London 1923
Petronii Arbitri Satyricon cum apparatu critico edidit Konrad Müller, München 1961

Petronii Cena Trimalchionis, herausgegeben von Helmut Schmeck, vierte, neu-
bearbeitete und verbesserte Auflage (Sammlung Vulgärlateinische Texte)
Heidelberg 1954
Petronii Arbitri Satiricon cum uberioribus commentarii instar, notis, Johannes
A. Woweren, Amsterodami 1626
*Priapeia sive Diversorum Poetarum in Priapum Lusus; illustrati Commentariis
Gasperis Schoppi, Franci; L. Apulii Madavrensis, Anexomenos ab eodem il-
lustratus etc. etc.* Patavii 1664
Petronius, The Satyricon and the Fragments translated with an introduction by
John Sullivan, London 1965

OTHER WORKS

Abbott, Frank Frost, "The Use of Language as a means of characterisation in
Petronius", C.P. 2, 1907, 43–50
Arnold, E. V., *Roman Stoicism*, London 1911
Bagnani, G., "Arbiter of Elegance", *Phoenix* Suppl. 2, Toronto 1954
Bickel, E., "Petrons Simplicitas bei Tacitus" *Rheinisches Museum* 90, 1941,
269ff.
Barré, see Roux
Bogner, H, "Petronius bei Tacitus" *Hermes* 76, 1941, 223*f.*
Bucheit, V., "Studien zum Corpus *Priapeorum*", *Zetemata* Hft. 22, München
1962
Bürger, K., "Der Antike Roman vor Petronius", *Hermes*, 27, 1892, 345 *ff.*
Cichorius, C., *Römische Studien*, Berlin 1922
Clarke, G. W., "The Burning of Books and Catullus 36", *Latomus* XXVII, 1968,
575ff.
Courtney, E., "Parody and Literary Allusion in Menippean Satire", *Philologus*
102, 1/2 1962, 86–100
Dudley, D. R., *A History of Cynicism*, London 1937
Durkheim, E., *Suicide*, (trans. Spaulding, Simpson), Glencoe, Illinois, 1951
Duff, J. W., *Freedmen in the Early Roman Empire*, Cambridge repr. 1958
Duff, J. W., *Roman Satire*, Cambridge 1937
Elliott, R. C., *The Power of Satire*, Princeton 1960
Fowler, Ward W., *The Religious Experience of the Roman People*, London 1911
Geiger, K. A., *Der Selbstmord im Klassischen Altertum*, Augsburg 1888
George, P., "Style and Character in the *Satyricon*", Arion V, 1966, 336–358
Heinze, R., "Petron und der Griechischen Roman", *Hermes* XXXIV 1899, 494–
519
Henderson, B. W., *The Life and Principate of the Emperor Nero*, London 1903
Herter, H., *De Priapo*, Giessen 1932
Highet, G., "Petronius the Moralist", *T.A.P.A.* 1941, 179–194
Hirzel, R., *Der Dialog* (repr.), Hildesheim 1963
Hirzel, R., *Der Selbstmord* (*Archiv für Religionswissenschaft* 1906), repr. Darm-
stadt 1967
Hoïstad, R., *Cynic Hero and Cynic King*, Uppsala 1948
Kerenyi, K., *Die Griechisch-Orientalische Romanliteratur in Religionsgeschichtlicher
Beleuchtung*, Tübingen 1927
Killeen, J. F., "James Joyce's Roman Prototype", *Comparative Literature* IX
3, 1957, 193–203
Klebs, E., "Zur Composition von Petronius' Satirae", *Philologus* 47, 1889, 623–
635

Kroll, W., *Studien zum Verständnis der Römischen Literatur*, Darmstadt (repr.) 1959
Latte, K., *Römische Religionsgeschichte* (Handbuch der Altertumswissenschaft), München 1960
Luck, G., *Latin Love Elegy*, London 1959
MacKendrick, Paul, "The Great Gatsby and Trimalchio", *Classical Journal* 45, 7, 1950, 304–314
Marx, F. A., "Tacitus und die Literatur der exitus illustrium virorum", *Philologus* XLVI, 1937, 83–103
Perry, B. E., *The Ancient Romances, A Literary-Historical Account of their Origins*, (Sather Classical Lectures) California 1967
Raith, O., *Petronius Ein Epikureer*, Erlangen 1963
Reich, H., *Der Mimus*, Berlin 1903
Rini, A., *Petronius in Italy*, N.Y. 1937
Rohde, E., *Der Griechische Roman*, Hildesheim 1960
Rose, K. F. C., "The Author of the Satyricon", *Latomus* XX, 1961, 811–825; "The Date of the Satyricon", *C.Q.* NS XIII, 1, 1962, 166–168; "Problems of Chronology in Lucan's Career", *T.A.P.A.* XCVII 1966, 379–396; "Time and Place in the Satyricon", *T.A.P.A.* XCIII 1962, 402–9; "The Petronian Inquisition, an Auto-da-Fé", *Arion* 1966, 275–301.
Roux, H., Barré, M.L., *Herculaneum et Pompeii, Recueil Général des Peintures, Bronzes, etc.* Paris 1872
Solonius, A. H., "Die Griechen und das Griechische in Petrons Cena Trimalchionis". *Societas Scientiarum Fennica Commentationes Humanarum Literarum* II, 1, 15. Helsingfors 1927
Sayre, F., *Diogenes of Sinope, A Study of Greek Cynicism*. Baltimore 1938
Schnur, H. C., "The Economic Background of the Satyricon", *Latomus* 18, 1959, 790 ff.
Stanford, W. B., "Ulyssean Qualities in Leopold Bloom", *Comparative Literature* 5, 1953, 125–136; *The Ulysses Theme*, Oxford 1954
Stengel, E., *Suicide and Attempted Suicide*, London 1964
Sullivan, J. P., *The Satyricon of Petronius, A Literary Study*, London 1968
Stubbe, H., "Die Verseinlagen im Petron", *Philologus* Suppltbd. 25, Leipzig 1925
Syme, R., *Sallust*, California 1964; *Tacitus*, Oxford 1958; *The Roman Revolution*, Oxford 1939
Todd, F. A., *Some Ancient Novels*, Oxford 1940
Toynbee, A., *Hannibal's Legacy*, Oxford 1965
Wagenwoort, H., *Roman Dynamism*, Oxford 1947
Wilkinson, L. P., "Philodemus and Poetry", *G. & R.* 2, 1933, 144ff.
Wissowa, G., *Religion und Kultus der Römer*, München 1912
Zeller, E., *Philosophie der Griechen*, ed. 5. Darmstadt 1963

CITATIONS OF THE TEXT OF THE *SATYRICON*

INDEX

In recent years there has been a closer examination of those aspects of Petronius' fragmentary satirical novel that go far beyond the problems presented by his language and style.

In *Petronius the Artist,* this critical activity is taken into account and utilised in the investigation of a number of themes which cast some light both on the novel itself and on the personality and artistic character of its author.

An attempt is made to take a fresh look at the portrayal of character in the novel, and it is suggested that the characters, even the minor ones, are much more well-rounded and human than has usually been conceded, and that they gain in satirical impact because they are not merely satirical lay-figures; also, the influence on Petronius' work of the portrayal of character in ancient epic is discussed. The posture of the novel in relation to its contemporary environment has often been debated: *Petronius the Artist* approaches this question by an investigation of the numerous *loci* in which pretence and concealment occur in the novel. It is clear that the novelist was profoundly aware of the gap that lies between words and actions.

The Priapus theme which has been regarded as important in the architecture of the *Satyricon,* is discussed in a broad context. The "biographical" notice of Petronius in Tacitus' *Annales* is examined, and it is suggested that according to Tacitus (or his source) Petronius need not necessarily have been an actual participant in the most flagitious excesses that are attributed to Nero. Petronius was eventually suspected of being a rebel rather than a sophisticated jester and arbiter of elegance. This study considers him to be preeminently an artist, in the conduct of his life as well as in his novel. His satire is directed not so much against crude but essentially human personalities as against the painful and chaotic conditions of life in the First Century A.D., his attitude to the world in which he lived was not political but artistic, and this is to be seen not only in the surviving parts of his novel, but in the ironical artistry with which he arranged his own suicide. The study also compares synoptically the author of the *Satyricon* with three modern authors who have been supposed to have characteristics in common with him: James Joyce, Marcel Proust, and F. Scott Fitzgerald.

About the author: born in Ireland 1931; graduated at Trinity College Dublin 1954; Assistant Lecturer in Classics, Queen Mary College, University of London, 1955—58; Assistant Lecturer and Lecturer in Classics, University of Sheffield 1958—65; Foundation Professor and Chairman of Classical Studies, Monash University, Victoria, Australia, since 1965.